Echoing Song

Echoing Song

Contemporary Korean Women Poets

Edited by

Peter H. Lee

Korean Voices Series, Volume 8

White Pine Press   Buffalo, New York

Publication of this book was made possible, in part, by grants from the Daesan Foundation; the Witter Bynner Foundation for Poetry; the Sunshik Min Endowment for the Advancement of Korean Literature at the Korea Institute, Harvard University; with public funds from the New York State Council on the Arts, a State Agency, and by the National Endowment for the Arts, which believes that a great nation deserves great art.

NATIONAL
ENDOWMENT
FOR THE ARTS

Printed and bound in the United States of America.

First Edition

ISBN 1-893996-35-2

Library of Congress Control Number: 2005920856

Published by
White Pine Press
P.O. Box 236
Buffalo, New York 14201
www.whitepine.org

Contents

Preface

To date there has been no anthology of modern Korean women's poetry, either in Korean or in any western language. *The Silence of Love: Twentieth-Century Korean Poetry* (Honolulu: University of Hawaii Press, 1980) contains representative poems of sixteen major Korean male poets from Han Yongun (1879–1944) to Kim Chiha (b. 1941), but no woman poet.

Now, I have compiled and edited an anthology of contemporary Korean women's poetry that reflects the achievements of women poets— each with an independent female identity. With the assistance of Professor Kim Chôngnan of Sangji University, a leading poet and feminist critic, I have chosen twenty contemporary women poets who have been active from the 1970s to the present.

I asked each of the eighteen poets still living to choose representative poems from her published work that demonstrate her poetic development, her concerns, and the poetic world she inhabits. Thus, this anthology demonstrates the originality and variety of modern Korean women's poetry with a selection that is rich in complex patterns of thought, feeling, and verbal resonance. Many poems present a distinctly feminine discourse with its own structure and diction and a consciousness emerging from feminine experience.

Korean women continue to suffer from gender inequality and sexual discrimination due to a patriarchal culture, the advance of industrialization/capitalism, and a gendered language system. Korea's social and academic environment is intolerant of feminism, considering it a Western ideology and perceives gender issues as insignificant in comparison to class and nationalist issues. Women poets have abjured the label "feminist" and take a much more subtle approach to gender-related issues. This is more indicative of a resistance to patriarchal constructions of femininity than a rejection of feminism. Some articulate a Korean feminism that stands opposed to colonial, patriarchal, economic, and cultural oppression. They offer varying critiques of such oppression and repression through the development of complex subjectivities that both reflect and contest gender-related inequities. Though under-appreciated, they have enjoyed a contemporary renaissance, which indicates that indirect resistance is difficult for patriarchal authorities to control.

Despite the hostile ideological environment, Korean women poets have explored a feminine diction to express female experience from a female perspective. Questioning the symbolic basis of women's social oppression, the language of these poets is marked by the inflections of gender—especially musicality, sound symbolism, openness, indirection, irony, and uncontrollable energy and laughter—and their experience informs their artistic vision. Delving into a female poetic tradition in the canon—including anonymous poets and singers of earlier times, female entertainers who wrote both in literary Chinese and in the vernacular, singers of *p'ansori*, and shamans' narrative chants—they have succeeded in constructing a modern female voice of resistance that does not neglect women's spousal and maternal role.

An introductory essay, which first appeared as "Late Twentieth-Century Poetry by Women" in *A History of Korean Literature*, ed. Peter H. Lee (Cambridge: Cambridge University Press, 2003), is reprinted with the permission of Cambridge University Press. Headnotes in which each poet explains "Why I Write" will help the reader to place the poet in context and understand her work. Bibliographical notes provide a short biography and the published works of each poet.

I wish to express my thanks to the poets for answering my questions, the translators for their willingness to undertake the difficult task, the Daesan Foundation for their support of this project, and Elaine LaMattina for her helpful suggestions.

—Peter H. Lee

Introduction

Today, more than ever before, Korean women poets are cultivating a determined voice all their own. Their works are diverse and their ability is impressive. Indeed, their literary achievement surpasses that of "men's poetry" in quantity and quality to such an extent that classifying "women's poetry" as a separate genre seems embarrassing.

Although the problem of establishing exactly when Korean women's poetry originated leaves room for discussion, scholars generally view women poets who became active around the 1920s as the pioneers. This was when Korean society was transformed from authoritarianism to enlightenment and Koreans experienced a radical change of consciousness. Yet the change in women was even more radical than in men—it was a case of vertigo. Women poets who initiated a certain "realistic" revolution not only in their work but also in their lives can be regarded as its extreme manifestation.

THE FIRST WAVE

If we divide modern Korean women's poetry into periods for the sake of discussion, the first wave of poets would include Kim Myôngsun (1896–1951), Kim Wônju (1896–1971), Na Hyesôk (1896–1946), and others. These women are celebrated more for their lives than for their work: Kim Myôngsun is said to have suffered from delirium; Kim Wônju and Na Hyesôk converted to religion after scandalous extramarital affairs. Judging from the sentiment of Korean society, where adultery is still a crime, one can easily imagine how deviant their behavior must have seemed at the time. To today's literary sensibility, this first period of women's poetry seems naive and not very prolific. Still, keeping in mind the tenor of society at the time, these women's thirst for independence and recognition of repression is extraordinary.

Women poets active during the 1930s left a richer body of work than the first wave, but they suffered from the criticism leveled at their predecessors. Unlike the pioneers, who were independently active, they began their writing careers under the "guidance and care" of male writers. Thus, although they secured a position in the literary world, they were hindered in expressing their female identity. This circumstance prevailed almost until the 1960s. Nevertheless, during this period Korean women poets were able to polish their technique and develop their literary ability. If there was no great progress toward the recognition of female identity, women's poetry did attain independence from the liberation (1945) to the 1960s as women poets began to proliferate and their work grew in both quantity and quality. This period also saw the emergence of women poets who succeeded publicly, such as Kim Namjo (b. 1927), Hong Yunsuk (b. 1925), Hô Yôngja (b. 1938), and others who are still active. But although the women poets of this period made great progress in technical sophistication, surpassing the rough work of earlier poets, the self-conscious female identity in their work lags behind that of their predecessors. The principal emotion that pervades their poetic world is a sentimentalism that emphasizes "feminine passivity." Despite these limitations, and considering the inferior position of women in Korean society, their achievements are brilliant.

THE INVASION OF "FLESH"

The 1970s saw for the first time women's poetry in the genuine sense that secures both artistic achievement and an independent female identity. Kang Ûngyo (b. 1945) and Mun Chônghûi (b. 1947) had already mastered the technical sophistication of the poets of the 1960s. In addition, they were the first women poets to recognize the meaning of "being women" in ontological and social terms. The peculiar separatist label of "female" that contemptuously followed women of letters began to disappear around this time—due largely to the activity of these two poets. But the literary changes were not limited to women's poetry. In the 1970s Korean literature experienced a radical change in quantity and quality. There were several reasons for this. First was the emergence of the *hangûl* generation, who had received a proper education in pure vernacular and were trained to write—unlike the previous generation, who had been educated under Japanese colonialism. Second was the expansion of modernization. This was the period when Koreans secured, above all, a citizen's consciousness. After liberation, despite unprecedented political chaos, slowly they began to acquire an outlook that enabled them to participate as subjects in historical development. The student revolution of April 19, 1960 represented a decisive point in the formation of this consciousness. Third was the burst of publication activity. Sudden economic expansion not only provided the crux of Korea's stability but also mass-produced numerous contradictions. This state of affairs stirred an urgent resistance in the intellectuals; and it created the media: *Munhak kwa chisông* (Literature and Intellect), *Ch'angjak kwa pip'yông* (Creation and Criticism), and other journals were founded. Literature became a key cultural and social strategic point of the intellectuals' resistance. And as the volume of publication increased, the opportunity to publish was extended to women poets.

These changes exerted a direct influence on Korean women's poetry. The formation of a citizen's consciousness spurred the growth of self-identity even in women. The themes and images that appear in the early work of Kang Ûngyo and Mun Chônghûi, who became active during the 1970s, are surprisingly similar despite the clear differences in their dispositions. The common points that link the early poems of these two women converge on the word "flesh" *(sal)*. From this word alone it can be seen that they pursued a female identity clearly distinct from the previous generation of women poets. Even as late as the 1960s, a woman evoking her own body in poetry, not conceptually but existentially, was unimaginable. I cannot forget my shock, for example, when I first read the word "flesh" in Kang Ûngyo's poem—the word "flesh," not "body." Flesh that exults and grieves, flesh that emits fragrance and stench. Flesh that is born and decays. Flesh that civilization has decreed as women's lot, that has been sent to the hell of the other, together with women, in order to maintain the predominance of mind. It is difficult to believe that Kang Ûngyo and Mun Chônghûi were consciously aware of the meaning of this word when they were writing. They moved intuitively, recognizing anew what the metaphysics of men repressed most in women: their bodies.

We can give a more immediate meaning to the word "flesh." Although these two poets reveal a self-consciousness concerning the female condition in a universal sense, in the context of Korean society the word has a far more active meaning. The 1970s were a time when political oppression represented by "Yusin"[1] was rampant. All the critical voices denouncing dictatorship were silenced. Korean society was crushed under a heavy atmosphere of death and oppression. The "flesh" of Kang Ûngyo and

17

Mun Chônghûi can be analyzed as a strategic code confronting this political oppression: flesh pulsating as the liveliest and immediate proof of innocence as opposed to political lies and pervasive death. While the male poets were pursuing modernism and ideology, Kang Ûngyo and Mun Chônghûi were hanging on to "flesh." They overcame the lie of the time by depending on flesh.

From People to Women

Korean women's poetry caught the pulse of positive change throughout the 1970s—from vague sentimentalism to philosophical subjects, from abstract diction to concrete discourse. The flow of this change becomes clearer after 1980 after the Kwangju Uprising at the beginning of the 1980s. Korean literature, in agony from oppression throughout the 1970s, was now thrust into an even darker tunnel. And as the political situation grew worse, poets were forced to respond. To confront a corrupt reality, one must possess the power to analyze it meticulously. The poets, therefore, armed themselves with an intense historical consciousness. Throughout the 1970s the currents of literary change had been integrated with the flow of realism. But beneath the main current were smaller tributaries soon to become major streams.

Ko Chônghûi (1948–1991) was active in the mid-1980s, before other poets, for precisely these reasons. She was clearly distinguished from other women poets because of her consciousness of reality. Before turning to literature, she had studied theology. In her early poems, Christianity is associated with liberation. In one sense, her literature can be seen as a means to practice her faith: working for the liberation of the people. Certainly her literary efforts were always faithful to the major goal of integrating life and literature. After the middle period, Ko Chônghûi's poetic activity moved toward integrating *minjung* (people) liberation and women's liberation. This change related to her insight that social alienation is exemplified in the problem of women. Recognizing that even within their socioeconomic "class" women are alienated—and recognizing too that if female alienation is not solved, even *minjung* liberation will become a fabricated ideology—made her a combative women's rights activist. She published a women's newspaper on her own, organized the feminist association Another Culture, and plunged into publication, among other activities. In June 1991 she met her death while climbing Mount Chiri—a profoundly symbolic and meaningful end.

DEATH AND MATERNITY

The political corruption of the 1980s that began with the Kwangju Uprising continued with the unprecedented abolition of free speech. Intellectual journals encountered heavy frost. The liberal literary camp, represented by the journal *Literature and Intellect,* and the realist literary camp, represented by *Creation and Criticism,* formed a united front despite their differences of tone and literary aim. The liberals took part in this combat with "deconstructionist poetry," an exceptional formal aestheticism. And among women poets, Ch'oe Sûngja (b. 1952) was the frontrunner.

Ch'oe Sûngja attacked corrupt society with corrupt language. In her work there is no trace of the gentility and elegance once considered "feminine." Instead there is rough and urgent breathing, vulgarity, and curses—a far cry from the pretty "female *(yôryu)* poetry" of the 1960s. But this rough language itself has no intrinsic meaning. The poet's shrewd spirit of denial has methodically mobilized it; in order to attack duplicity, she has chosen these words strategically. Her poems aroused interest from the time of her debut and were loved by many, and not only because women were able to experience catharsis through them. In her poems women discovered the possibility of a new, independent feminism different from anything that had preceded it: that of a sorceress on her own; a woman stranded in dignity; a powerful, subjective, unfortunate woman—not a pretty princess who is the object of men.

That same spirit of denial drove Yi Yônjů (1953–1992) to suicide. Yi began to publish in the late 1980s. After publishing her first volume of poetry in 1991, she took her life. Although she can be seen as a poet of the 1990s in terms of chronology, we must discuss her together with Ch'oe Sûngja because their poetic spirits seem to touch. And, I think, after Ch'oe Sûngja's tragedy and Yi Yônju's suicide, women poets of the late 1980s and the 1990s were able to construct a rich and self-sufficient female poetic world. Yi Yônju's first collection is titled *Night Market with Prostitutes* (Maeûmnyô ka innûn sijang). The choice of the word "prosti-

19

tute" is itself profound: it indicates that the poet's self-identity was suffering from a confusion sufficiently violent for her to choose the ultimate solution.

In order to understand Yi Yônju's breakdown, one must understand the crux of her problem: the city and a civilization of patriarchy. The "city" is not only the pinnacle of patriarchal cultural glory but also an evil setting. Yi Yônju exposes its contradiction; she identifies with the prostitute—an unfortunate woman, at the city's periphery, who cannot be incorporated into the system. The prostitute is a product of urbanization and one of the most brazen contradictions of a patriarchal civilization whose double standard of monogamy is only a façade. Yi Yônju's poems, centered on the prostitute's life, are full of the vocabulary of self-abasement. It seems that she attempts to incorporate into her identity what Sandra Lee Bartky calls a "horrible message of inferiority"[2] that is internalized in certain women with an evil intensity: the perfection of self-torture.

This indictment of women's otherness is not the result of passively accepting the colonization accorded women in a patriarchal society. It involves pain that must be overcome if women are to construct a true identity—to borrow Ch'oe Sûngja's words, "in order to be born again." It urges women to recognize their condition, to stand on their own, to rage against oppression. Indeed, the "liberation of rage" is a major stage of women's consciousness raising. And in the case of Yi Yônju, rage devoured a poet.

Insightful Mothers

Kim Sûnghûi (b. 1952) and Kim Hyesun (b. 1955), however, conquered women's otherness with a definite social consciousness and blissful maternity. The beginning of Kim Sûnghûi's poetic career in the early 1970s was distinguished by her pursuit of the mythological world. Her early poems—like those of many young poets—are idealistic but display undeniable talent. She quickly overcame her early idealism and turned to cultural criticism in the late 1980s. Her early mythological imagination is not given its proper place because of the strong wind of realism that rushed in immediately afterward. But this gifted poet did not break down; even in her despair, she developed her poetic world. By the end of the 1980s, that world had become the subject of widespread attention, and she enjoyed the rare good fortune of winning a literary award.

From her debut, Kim Hyesun indiscriminately attacked men's dark rigor with her lively imagination. Even in her later work, her imagination is still novel and fresh. She possesses a sharp perception that penetrates the political meaning of the "act of discourse." This keen perception links Kim Sûnghûi and Kim Hyesun and is confirmed by the fact that they are among the first women poets to steadily publish exceptional prose on poetry. Kim Hyesun is a contemporary of Ch'oe Sûngja who began her literary career in the 1980s, but because of her diction she has more in common with new generations of poets than with her contemporaries. She does not so much present the content of her poem as convey its expression. Thus she exploits a sophisticated technique of making the "act of discourse" itself an internally meaningful poetic strategy. From the first, her poems grasp the conspiracy of patriarchy. This insight does not allow her to settle for monotonous diction. She hits and runs. Unlike Ch'oe Sûngja and Kim Sûnghûi, who in a singular and direct way criticize the male value system that oppresses them, Kim Hyesun uses diverse methods—parody, black humor, material images, and dialogical technique—to express the existence of the other: the other that is introduced into the domain of the self to criticize the absoluteness of the subject, the basis of male metaphysics. She moves freely in all directions. Her diversity, however, sometimes has the effect of blurring her poetic intent by blinding the reader with exquisite technique.

Kim Sûnghûi and Kim Hyesun have a definite consciousness insofar as the question of identity is concerned. Beginning with Kang Ûngyo and Mun Chônghûi, and continuing through Ko Chônghûi and Ch'oe Sûngja, one can say that the meaning of "being a woman" was revealed. But Kim Sûnghûi and Kim Hyesun—self-conscious of substantial, affirmative, and independent maternity—leaped over the dimension of Kang's and Mun's inclusive meaning of "flesh," Ko's ideological democratic feminism, and Ch'oe's indictment of female rage through the recognition of otherness based on lack. In the background was the feminist activity that began in Korean society in the 1980s.

Essentially the 1980s ended with the president's declaration of June 29, 1987 and the Seoul Olympics.[3] A change began to accelerate in Korean literature. Lightness rather than heaviness, individuality rather than totality, become its center. In women's poetry, a change occured also. Due to the successes of the first half of the 1980s, almost all the taboos of women's poetry, taboos of poetic diction and the body, disappeared. Female poets in the latter half of the 1980s were able to use uninhibited expressions and exhibit their own bodies. Even their own sexual desire was talked about naturally. The "woman as sexual subject," whom even Mun Chônghûi—who did not hide the bodily functions—perceived with a guilty conscience has now become an everyday theme in Korean women's poetry. Women poets no longer consider their sex as an obstacle. In a certain sense, it can even be said that being a woman is advantageous for writing. (In fiction this is definitely true.)

But examining the issue more closely, we find that almost nothing has changed. After a meticulous analysis of the 1980s reactionary movement, literary authorities have driven women's poetry into a corner with a very subtle formula. The deconstructionists (dissident postmodernists using open forms) active during the 1980s swept most of the literary awards and were heralded as stars. The conservative literary authorities, however, were consistently critical. Their main complaint was that "deconstructionist poetry" was ruining traditional lyricism. Although popular support and the serious evaluation of young critics helped to quiet this criticism, the literary authorities denied recognition of Ch'oe Sûngja, who was among the "deconstructionist poets," until the end.

One can guess why literary men cheered the reactionary women's poetry that came out during the latter half of the 1980s. This restoration, or reaction, was a phenomenon not only in women's poetry but also in men's; it is very significant in that it regained some of the lyricism that poetry lost when it was mobilized as an instrument of combat against social corruption in the 1980s. "Ah, we are exhausted from fighting. Poetry, console us. You especially, women poets, console us men." Men abandoned their battlefield colleagues and returned to find their women. The female identity revealed by the poetry of Hô Sugyông (b. 1964) and Pak Nayôn (b. 1951), two women poets who were praised by literary men in the late 1980s, seems to play this role. The title of the volume that made Pak Nayôn famous is suggestive: *Princess P'yônggang Who Lives in Seoul* (*Sôul e sanûn P'yônggang kongju*). Princess P'yônggang, who marries the idiot Ondal and transforms him into a great warrior with absolute devotion, represents the traditional female image. Hô Sugyông displays a charming femininity and presents herself as a consoler of the menfolk returning from the violent battles of the 1980s.

Two other women who started publishing poems at the same time present a feminine self that is acceptable to men. Hwang Insuk's poetry has images of the "girl" and Yi Chinmyông's offers the "chaste wife." Compared to their earlier work, however, their current poems do not show much development. It appears they could not muster the courage to smash the female image that is comfortable to men—an image that has been, to a degree, the cause of these poets' success. Hwang Insuk (b. 1958) failed to mature, and Yi Chinmyông (b. 1955) could not pull herself from the depths of the interior, the religious speculation evoked by emotion, and shows a tendency to cling to dogma. (In her poetry it appears in the image of Scripture. The problem is that she does not show what is in the Scripture, just the external image.) Her poetry stretches and lengthens but fails to gain density. She loiters at one place, unable to leave, and to explain the reason for her loitering she becomes talkative.

One cannot deny the literary accomplishment of these four women. Their poems are indeed well written. Hô Sugyông's poems display deft diction and shape a decadent beauty in the indigenous tunes of the Korean language. Hwang Insuk's fresh poetry constructs a sophisticated urban aestheticism. Yi Chinmyông, with severely decorous and virtuous language, steps toward a religious speculation that is rare in Korean literature. Yet they do have their limitations. Unless female poets can resist aesthetic accommodation, true women's literature is impossible.

Today's Generation

A number of the "middle-aged women poets" have secured their position. Given the Korean literary world's practices, however, their chances of survival are slim. They are the "destitute of language" who lack the customary links to elite Korean society: having attended certain schools; a specific regional background; knowing the right people. They all made their literary debut at a very late age, experienced acute psychological distress during their youth, and are groping for deliverance through literature. (One suspects that this distress was the result of the forcible repression of their literary talent. Despite their late start, their talent is prodigious.)

Their appearance can be explained not only in terms of their personal history but also in terms of Korean literary history. They entered the scene in the postmodernist 1990s, when self-narrative that could not be expressed in the 1980s rose to the surface as resourcefulness was being restored to literature. Given these circumstances it seems almost a miracle that these poets were read with interest. That women who embark upon a literary career after a certain age are labeled "middle-aged women poets" is the reality of the Korean literary world.

Three of these women are publishing at an astonishing rate. Concentrated by the urgency of life they have repressed, and by their thirst for a language that was alienated by patriarchal values, their poems explode from their interiors. Indeed, their poetry is fresher and more energetic than that of most young poets. Male poets of the same age, by contrast, simply repeat similar matter and manner. Yi Kyôngnim (b. 1947) exploits a language that is a mix of Ch'oe Sûngja's and Hô Sugyông's, with inborn talent and a powerful sense of female identity. She writes almost in gasps—so repressed that, having gained an outlet, sometimes she tries to speak too urgently. In her latest poems, she manipulates a more diverse breathing technique, as if she has acquired confidence. Pak Sôwôn (b. 1960) is another poet with a seething interior. Her poems offer striking images and an intense and confessional narrative that recalls the poetry of Sylvia Plath (1932–1963) or Anne Sexton (1928–1974). With its gorgeous yet ferocious images and primitive religious sentiment, her work exudes an odd sacrilegious air. Yi Hyangji (b. 1942), the oldest of the three, exploits a language that is severe in self-censorship and concealed under layer after layer. But in fact her "tied tongue" is a poetically meaningful device. Among the three, she writes the most daring and successful poems.

We turn now to Kim Chôngnan (b. 1953), who made her debut in the 1970s, and Chông Hwajin (b. 1959), who published her first poetry collection in the 1980s. Poets of the 1990s, they have created a poetic world with a distinct character. Although they accept the achievements of 1980s women's poetry, they diverge from it. The pivotal point of this change is present in Kim Hyesun's work. If Kim Hyesun is looking for "you" to dissolve the old self and construct a new one, exploring the true identity of this "you" is the main thrust of Korean women's poetry in the 1990s.

The women of this generation seem to grasp the contemporary mission of women's poetry as constructing a new ontology instead of indicting feminine otherness or rejecting social constraints. The ontology that invites "you" is ultimately the ontology that restores the other, whom the philosophy of male self-identity has shoved into oblivion. Consequently, if this generation of women poets wants to talk about "love," it is appropriate. This love is very far from the "love" in poems mass-produced by Korean women poets of the 1960s. It is not the romantic love so despised by feminists nor is the passive love that tries to make up for social inferiority by offering a self-sacrifice for men. It is, rather, an act of searching for a new identity constructed by demolishing the old frame of existence. It is an act of being united with the flow of life in the flux of the universe. These poets no longer feel pain being women. Their feminine identity is now a beacon of their pride: a mark of conviction that they did not side with power or serve power. In order to practice this ontology, the current generation of Korean women poets is slowly entering the deep recesses of the soul, still an unexplored realm. Already they have conquered new territory. While men agonize over the surface world's aridity, Korean women are pushing open the door of the unconscious and calmly walking barefoot the waterway that Rimbaud had not finished at the end of the nineteenth century.

Their poetic world reveals the possibility of a new metaphysics we might call "self-religion." From deep within they are quietly resurrecting a spiritual immediacy that religion lost when it began to lean on reason and institutions. It has nothing to do with this or that doctrine; it is not a matter of religion but a problem of religiosity. These poets seem to know where their ontology is headed. They seem prepared to accept the postmodernist "pursuit of religiosity" as theirs. The reason why this summons came not to novelists but to poets—especially women poets— is, paradoxically, because poetry, especially women's poetry, is the most powerless literary genre in Korean society. Consequently, it has the least exchange value, is least corrupted by commercialism, and is the farthest removed from the grand symbolic framework of postmodern society. This point is crucial. After all, the problem of writing poetry in modern society is securing a pure language that can withstand all the symbolic manipulation. And Korean women poets, especially the current generation, are all sensitive to the problem of language and clearly understand the political meaning of the "act of discourse."

—Kim Chôngnan

1. "Yusin" was a "revitalizing" project announced by Park Chung Hee in 1972. The same word was used in Japan for the Meiji Restoration. See Carter J. Eckert, Ki-baik Lee, et al., *Korea Old and New: A History* (Seoul: Ilchokak, Publishers for Korea Institute, Harvard University, 1990), p. 365.
2. Sandra Lee Bartky, *Femininity and Domination: Studies in the Phenomenology of Oppression* (New York: Routledge, 1990).
3 A bold "eight-point program of reform" was announced by President Roh Tae Woo. See Eckert, et al., *Korea Old and New*, p. 382.

Translators

The translator's initials follow each translated poet.

AC - Ann Y. Choi, Rutgers University
AK - Aimee N. Kwon, University of California, Los Angeles
CK - Catherine J. Kim, University of California, Los Angeles
CS - Carolyn U. So, formerly with Claremont McKenna College
JL - Jennifer M. Lee, University of California, Los Angeles
JP - Julie C. Park, Deep Springs College
KR - K. Kim Richards, University of California, Berkeley
MH - Mickey Hong, University of California, Los Angeles
PL - Peter H. Lee, University of California, Los Angeles
SR - Steffen F. Richards, Berkeley, CA
YK - Yung-Hee Kim, University of Hawaii at Manoa
YR - Youngju Ryu, University of California, Los Angeles

Echoing Song

Yi Hyangji
(b. 1942)

Why I Write

I was born, grew up, got married, and now I'm getting old. I'm a woman, a Korean woman, an open sore. For a long time I didn't love myself. In a last attempt to love myself again, I chose poetry. I hadn't been loved, not even by myself, and I wanted to give myself a chance to speak out. I also wanted to give myself an answer that could lead me to conclude that birth is a blessing, not a curse. Moreover, I longed to develop a landscape of my own, free of all obligations and traditions.

Sunrise

Blood stolen from my body before dawn
soars, tears the horizon!

The pain of some fifty years, salted by darkness,
hangs in the eastern sky;
it sure looks round!

Trees of night stand next to it, shaking in the wind.
Arranging flowers that will die by dawn,
it dyes the entire mountain red.

Let's go! Let's go!
Dawn is resurrected, like Medusa.

Leaf Struck by Bird Droppings

Before the leaf could shake off the bird droppings,
autumn, early, arrived.

Not knowing their sin,
the birds left droppings, then rose toward the sky
while the tree tried to drop the heaviest leaf first.

Let's fall, let's fall,
I think, trembling.
All right, let's fall!

From the ignorance and wandering of spring days,
from the rage and sorrow of summer days,
from the last bell of the cruel season...

I'll think about it,
bathed in the eternal flame:
What makes my arms bend toward bird droppings?

What Did You Do Yesterday?

—What did you do yesterday?
—I cried for the first time. My mom's voice, which used to carry a lull-aby through the long cord connected to my belly button, suddenly turned into the shriek of a torn drum, and some unknown hand ruth-lessly spanked my butt.

—What did you do yesterday?
—I lay down in the grassy field. Children from my grandpa's village sur-rounded me and made me look at a boy's weenie. The blue sky was get-ting higher and higher, the grass poked my back under my thin clothes, and until the big sister from the village shooed the children away, I lis-tened to the cries of the flock of crows.

—What did you do yesterday?
—I walked in a seaweed village under the sea. The tiny moon called out to me, rustling the water's surface. I popped out of the water, struggling to catch the moon. The sea rose high in front of me, the wave stood like a wall at my back. From the right, from the left, waves dashed, wearing steel gloves. Moonlight scattered on my head like fragments of porce-lain.

—What did you do yesterday?
—I stood in the wind. The wind flipped the thorn tree's branch, which grabbed my hair. I cut that branch, dangling like a spider, off. My palms became a sunset, scarlet with my blood.

—What did you do yesterday?
—I bid farewell to a single maiden. I spread a silk cloth with rainbow hues under her feet while she walked, trembling, toward a better place, the place where she no longer hears the cry of waves that bite off rocks when the wind blows.

—What did you do yesterday?
—I buried all women and humiliation under ground. One mountain

lowered its shoulder and accepted my unexpected graves. Now is the time to lie down silently and become the mountain's flesh. Ah, ah, but I can't deny that my mind is a dance of crimson earth flying in the wind.

The March of Dawn

This dawn I completely lost my face.
I'd been long awake, but as though I were a breathing sack,
I simply watched it vanishing, indulging in lingering sleep.

Afraid of waking the buds of darkness,
I simply stared at the marching faces floating above my face,
at those transparent masks leaving endless steps behind.

Mere spectator, I couldn't even scream while losing myself,
the hand of darkness so tender I didn't feel the plunderer's claws,
didn't even realize what they were.

At dawn I looked blank, like a seven-year-old who's left home.
Inside the chimney, sparrows were deep in morning sleep;
draped windows were dying to see the rising sun.

Rising with my breath, vanishing into a higher darkness
like the afterglow that flickers in the earthworms' slime,
fading trail of fixed masks, where do you go?

What part of me rose with breaking dawn
and sent them from one darkness to another? I didn't call to them:
To be buried beneath their fragments is more frightening than their loss.

This dawn I lost those masks more precious than my face.
the masks I wasted my youth cleaning and pampering.
The wall of dawn collapsed; now I caress my bare and wrinkled face.

Acromatic Dawn

I'm a vane that wants to turn to the west./I'm a vane that wants to
turn to the east.
Why are you turning, hurting my wing?/Why are you turning,
hurting my wing?
Why are you copying me?/Why are you copying me?
You, crazy,/You, crazy,
The dawn of
the wings
breaks
from
out
si
d
e

In a corner, a giant mirror watches.

35

Reply at an Unknown Place

The sound of water in the shallows has stopped and now dry music
    flows.
I'm walking toward an unknown place, following a commanding
    voice.
I repeat the word "comfortable" three times, although I'm not.
The voice orders me to walk down the stairs, but there are none.
It tells me to grab a rail, but there isn't one.
While worrying about returning, I see a long wall on my right.

A white shadow-person hesitates on the stairs.
He descends the staircase, leaning to his right on the wall.
The voice tells me to look at the big bright door, but it isn't there.
It tells me to open the curtain and look out, but I see only black clouds
    swarming beneath the stairs.
It tells me to go and report what I've seen, but I haven't even
    finished descending the stairs.
It tells me to look at my hand; I see a woman's left hand, untouched
    by labor and sun.
The back of the hand looks too pale and lean.
It tells me to look at my foot; I see a woman's right foot, its back
    hardened by labor and sun.
It looks too dark, swollen, and rough.
It tells me to touch my face, but my hand doesn't feel a thing.
It asks me for the season; it's summer; it asks me for the year;
    350 floats vaguely up and down.
All the scenes are obscure; I'm worried about how to return.
Where am I? I see a gorge surrounded by fresh greenery; I see a
    woman standing
on the other side of the scarlet earth, dressed in a skirt
    and a jacket with its collar pulled up, putting both
    hands behind herself, as if carrying a baby on her back.

Her clothes are distressingly shabby, her crumbling face expressionless.
The voice tells me to look at this final face of her life, but I see only

the same lady whose feet face me, floating aslant.
It tells me to describe the lesson of her life—the word
          "submission" surfaces and is gone. Told to open my eyes,
I stop the tape recorder.

The loosely winding circles of the tape recorder have stopped.
My finger, so used to submissive machines—
Were those vague shadows the true images of submission?

Ringing in My Ears

A museum of pigs cries in my ears. Thanks to the pigs, I finished college. One pig per semester got kicked out of the house, got whipped instead of me.

 I cooked my own food in a house with a backyard people used for the illegal butchery of pigs. In the backyard behind my study, all those black pigs screamed and died. Drinking pork broth, I waited for a lover.

A huge sow seeps into my body like water, pulling my left shoulder down. "If your dream hurts you, open your eyes," said my father's voice. While drifting near the kitchen sink, I went to the river… Climbing down a wintery mountain, I hurt my left wrist.

As night returns, the black pigs also come back. The past won't release me. It's building a squealing museum in my ears,.

The Phoenix

It's flying in the wind,
pulling the branch of a silk tree taut.

The sound of wind
combed by jealous wings.

Strangled by indestructible sorrows,
the tree chokes,
pulling half of the future from a stony field.

At the edge of a lazy farmer's field
a vinyl bird still flaps its wings.
From its body, the tree gathers transformation's fiery seeds.

Leaving Home

Dad gave me a desk, Mom a bed
The desk is a relic of failure
The bed a rusty lullaby with loose springs

Dad gave me a name, Mom school expenses
The name of a child with many siblings is like a broken traffic light
Tuition a flower won by kneeling with cupped hands outside the door
        of bare existence

Dad gave me candy, Mom new clothes
The candy invited invisible worms into my teeth
The new clothes, once worn, turned to rags

Dad gave me a bag, Mom shoes
The bag has already grown old
The shoes, small

On the day a boat's horn blew, seagulls flew,
The sun frowned and waves danced,
The child left home in search of Seoul

The Joy of Love

Got married. As March rain stopped,
the sun of April's first day brought dreams of new anchorings
in the street of people and the harbor of ships. She and he,
      folded in each other's
arms, let loose two doves to heaven's vault.

From now on wherever the body goes, the mind should follow.
A woman is like a bamboo leaf shaking in wind;
a man gropes his way like a bamboo tree in fog.
The wounded body encloses like a forest the injured mind.

The day moonlight fades away like mint's scent arrives.
The doves flying in the sky are mixed with wine every night.
Duty won't descend from the bridge of the nose,
right wanders about underground, like a mole.

Fate rolls effortlessly on predetermined wheels;
love without hope carries ticks and mold.
The tree of promise sways in the wind;
Kaoliang endlessly fights the hands of time.

Thirty Aprils, without dance or song
brushed by the tree that flowers first and later puts out leaves.
The joy of love tossed into the closet.
I babble only of marriage's pain.

Song of a Balloon in Search of Her Mom's Balloon

I gave birth to two babies, aborted two, she grumbled for thirty-three years. Disgusted, her family left for other caves. Her task was to eat and sleep, eat and sleep, eat and sleep. The aborted babies returned to slumber's fragile jar: Let's carry Mom away; let's tear Mom to pieces. Bringing up Mom cost money, too. Once they'd escaped from sleep, the children, dripping with sweat, stood next to the dried laundry: Let's take Mom from the clothesline; let's fold Mom and put her in the dresser. Cleaning Mom cost money, too. Night and day, night and day, the chorus of the children. In sleep, in the rice bowl, the chorus of children. Let's hang Mom on a balloon and let her fly away. Dangling from a balloon, she left in search of her mom. Mom, Mom, she's wandering, looking for her mom's balloon.

The Sea

Ladies, why don't you lift a stone
and throw it at me?
I'm the mirror of time, your greatest fear.

As the children of clouds fell asleep inside petals,
Mom gave birth to me
in the washbasin of insomnia.

I'm the water thrown away in a desert
after washing Mom's bruised feet.
I hand down my fate.

The fish, morning and night,
lay eggs and semen constantly,
but only the jellyfish of confusion and separation
remain in fishermen's nets.... .

Ladies, why don't you lift a stone
and throw it at the future?
I'm the mirror of time, your greatest fear.

CK

No Hyangnim
(b. 1942)

Why I Write

Who am I? This question never fails to perplex me. I've been alone since childhood. No one taught me to be this way; I've always been lonely and lost in longing for something. I wanted to stand out from others and found pleasure in imagining what tasks might be infused with my identity or be true to my nature. Could this be what made me a poet?

I was alone, but I grew up near a seascape blessed by nature, so I wasn't entirely alone. I began to dream that there must be something beyond the ocean. The question of identity that had perplexed me was answered by the sea. The sounds of the waves were people's voices, and my keen senses, sharp as a whip, urged me on and made me the imagistic poet I am today.

How ecstatic I'll be if good poetry emerges from my life, even if that life is filled with suffering. This is how I'll lead the way toward better poetry. This is the reason I write. The meaning of my existence can be found only in poetry.

Dream

The sea was in front of me.
I'd always longed to see his face
embossed on a field of clay,
a house
where ghostly moaning emerged,
and sea pines
covering their bosoms
with hands like wire's scraps.

I longed for the scent of humans
while laid up with peritonitis
in a six-mat room
at a long corridor's end.

I longed to see
shattered porcelain, weeds, the smell of rubber,
a faint kerosene flame in the wind,
the stillness long buried in heaps
in the blacksmith's shop.
Ah! I longed to see
the sound of children flying around
on their hands and feet.

To pass the time,
I'd stroke the body of the sea.
When I awoke from my dream,
my mind was filled with only
dark stains of viscous saltiness.
The sea was always in front of me.

Windy Day

Beyond the riverbank, dredgers
poured out civilization.

In front, a road passed by.

From the sky,
granite pebbles
with laughing black mouths
spilled out.

A single burst of laughter floated down
the polluted river.

Wilted flowers,
impaled like sea foam
watched
from a black iron fence.

Black Hole

Autumn in Korea.
The day Stephen Hawking came,
unraveling twisted roads.

Leaves as bent as his body
greeted him while strands of his hair flew in the wind.
Leaves that couldn't get loose to greet him
thrashed around like the wings
of mighty birds

I don't know where that black hole is,
but I began to see it in Dr. Hawking's moist eyes
as he watched us through
his thick-rimmed glasses.

I don't know where that place is,
but everyone goes there alone.

Autumn Letter

How are you? It's autumn

Loose to the tips of my toes,
I flutter about
like a hazy light.

Like water,
like desolation,
like residue left underfoot.

With nothing to lean on, I constantly sneeze.
Discarding the destitute family,
worn furniture, and the one skeletal poem
I'd leaned on for so long,
I left the past behind.
Having done nothing, with no one to meet,
autumn and I are one,
pouring out of sunset sky dry rays of sun.
I gaze around
to see what else
has become of the autumn that's seeping away,
how it's yellowed and withered with me;
it's scattered in fields
or lying with me by trees
that irritate my weak lungs.
Although I look around,
there's only autumn.
What will be written, will be,
but one line of our suffering
will remain:
Good-bye!

Rooftop Violin

A man plays a violin on the roof.
Every day, the sound
rides our rooftop,
rises far into the sky,
where it becomes a stingray kite
with a glittering tail.

One day I went out on the veranda
and secretly cut the strings.
Before I could wind the spool,
something fell and shattered.
My bright future broke.
A few yards of sky shattered,
but someone still plays the violin.

A Country Where Snow Has Not Yet Fallen

A country where snow
has not yet fallen.
On one side,
evergreens moan,
holding out frozen hands.

The window rattles.
Snow invades
dreams left ajar,
and lonely people melt.

People deep in sleep
moan hot words
hidden inside each heart,
and the language of loneliness melts.

In sleep,
snowflakes touch,
pile up.

All for the sake of snow
that will fall tomorrow
or the next day.

Nature

In a corn field,
someone brandishes
a smart whip.

Ûh ûk...
Moonlight
severs at the waist
a shadow that kneels
as it slowly collapses.

Air passes, along with time,
into the sky where the sound of the whip
cuts through corn row after corn row,
plucking gossamer wings.

I bend my body
lightly, like
a transparent ballerina.

How will I float
to the sky?

Nursery

St. Peter's Hospital.
To the right of the entrance is the nursery.

In the mountain-ash forest
nearby
were many palm-size skies.

Three, four children
inside fragments of glass.

All took with them
skies close to their age.

Sunlight left behind,
alone,

three, four children
inside fragments of glass.

Yard

In the yard
where magnolia blossoms
tear like paper bags

I washed and hung
summer sheets.

The sky, under drought alert,
caught fire.

Sorrow burned without
even a spark

around the time
trees, severed at their roots,
swallowed their words.

Ap'ae Island 1—Diving Women

On clear days,
I can't see Ap'ae Island.
The women who live beyond the hill
go out with trowels and nets around their waists
and return
empty-handed
with skinned flesh and scratched thighs.
In the middle of the night
the frightening sea, contained,
becomes a hairy beast
and roars.
Where could he be? Bobbing around
an island no living person can see?
People who peek
through narrowed eyes
disappear without a trace.

Ap'ae Island 45—Once Upon a Time

Once upon a time, Ap'ae Island
was a field of clay.

The sea always longed for the mountain,
the mountain always longed for the sea.

The sound of waves
crossed the field of clay
and crawled toward the mountain.

Uru rung, uru rung
Kkwang kkwang
Kkooi kkooi

Rising slowly,
hills and boulders and bluffs
were formed.

That's why
the sound of waves
on Ap'ae Island
is particularly
fierce.

The village maidens, frightened,
all left for solid land.

Today the men of Ap'ae Island
lean once again toward the horizon
to cleanse their weary hearts.

AK

Ch'ŏn Yanghŭi
(b. 1942)

Why I Write

Although it earns me no food or money, I wrestle with poetry. Some people ridicule me: "Does your spirit sustain you?" In general, they're mad. Whatever anyone says, my response is that I write to live a good life, an enlightened life. Poetry is my life and my way.

Walking the road of humanity while learning about the world and awakening the self, isn't this what a good life is about? A road signifies the life process, the journey. When I write poetry, I search for answers to all things. In these moments I'm at once tormented yet find myself most natural and free.

Poetry won't grieve if I stop writing, but I will. If I stopped writing, I'd undoubtedly end up a wasteland. Externally my life may seem mundane, but inside I long to be beautiful and enlightened—even if it means that the brutality of life is increased by my intensity. If poetry is a temple raised with words, I'm a believer, and I devote myself to it.

Entering Chikso Falls

The sound of the waterfall awakens the mountain. Startled, a wild pheasant takes flight. A pine cone falls with a thud. A squirrel waves its tail, and the lonely trail is secretly illuminated.

Wa! It's the story of a *p'ansori* master, so familiar to my ears.

Kwanûm Mountain's summit is in front of me,
but I sense this place is the top.
How close the other world seems.
White pure land! I've always been a dreamer.

Mindless birds flew away, unpossessed,
White spray of Chikso Falls, a shining water palace.

The sound of the waterfall climbs the gorge. Like thunder, like a storm, like a standing ovation—boulders secretly tremble.

The sky is in front of me,
but I sense that this is the infinite void.
Coming here and gazing out,
how good the other world seems.

I'm relearning
a scene from a peerless master's performance.

Chikso Falls is a waterfall behind the Naeso Monastery in Pyônsan, North Chôlla. *P'ansori* masters often practiced near a waterfalls. When their voice could be heard above the sound of the water, they were ready to perform in public.

Millet Field in My Mind

A millet field passes through my mind again as I go to the backyard to
gather a few more butteburr leaves Something dark as dusk is also there.
     Right in front of my eyes,
     the evening star gazes down.
     When I let go of the world, I can't see a single path.
     At the end of the road, beyond rice paddy footpaths,
     is a field of barley,
     and years of harvests that ended the famines of spring.
     Wind beats against my back and the cancer-deep shadow of a
                    broken bone aches.
     Shaking and shaking my head,
     I see mountains amid mountains, with mountains above.
     I realize only now that I should look up.
     There, way over there, the sky is vibrant blue.
     The blue prods my shoulder—I must climb higher.
     As the pine breeze pushes me, desolation rises, too.
     My senses return in a flash. Each time they come back,
     the chirping of birds awakens me within.
     I can't take a path that doesn't exist.
     Circling the mountain, I climb its cliffs.
     Thousand Buddha Mountain
     enters my body and sits,
     brightening the millet field in my mind.

One Day

A few years ago, I was moved by a story
from Melbourne, Australia
about construction of a building
being suspended until a pair of peregrine falcons
that had nested and had chicks
atop the building flew away,
and I wondered when we could live such lovely lives.
I was shocked, as if by the miraculous,
by a story I saw in the newspaper the other day
about the construction of an apartment building
being suspended until a magpie
that had chicks
at the site flew away,
and this story that so moved me
was not from Melbourne but from our Seoul.
So this is the path attained by love,
the path of enlightenment.
Beauty and compassion can grow anywhere.
Today I finally entered the Hall of Peace.

Thoughts on a Bird

When I see a bird in a cage,
I see a woman in her house.
Her wings waste away; only her beak stays sharp.
This isn't living, she murmurs quietly.
Where on earth has the sky gone
that I can't reach it
no matter how hard I try?
Unbearably light, I long to fly,
but it's like life flung open the cage
and, to tell the truth, I'm afraid.
Beginnings, I know, are never easy.

Hummingbirds, smallest among birds,
even nameless mixed breeds,
all thrust their bodies toward the sky.
Yet you, blue-cheeked sparrow—
Ah! You can't. You shake your wings in the wind.
You'll be yourself
when you rise and fly away.
Find yourself, no matter what.
That's who you are.

Mountain Stroll

Passing by the swamp of cafés
in front of Tôksông Women's University,
I rest a moment under a zelkova tree
at the last station on Line 8
then cut across toward Nonduality Temple.
The roads I've walked were twisted,
and my feet seem to ache.
The labyrinth was a labyrinth from the start.
I believed that before I stopped searching,
everything would be as obvious as a forest.
With a rucksack on my back,
I stood like a tree behind a tree.
Now I know why the trees in this forest are so twisted,
covered by a forest's darkness even in midday.
When I scream as if to shatter the ridgeline,
even the darkness is comforting.
A journey bird quickly brushes past the branches,
and the sound of a bell scatters. . . .
While reading Lubis's *Twilight in Jakarta*[1]—
that teardrop flower!—Suyu soaks in dusk.

The hill path is too steep.
My own life, too, was a steep climb.
My friend rejected her home and even her true essence
to spend years of monthly rent, monthly rent, in the city.
        She, too, would have breathed heavily on this climb.
        Separate from the body, the mind descends,
        and the sound of water follows it down.
The temple can never be seen from the road.
It's always there at road's end
I push and enter the gate of Nonduality.
The main hall is under repair.
My broken spirit, fatigued for years,
cannot be restored.

My body, either hungry or longing for the fruit of immortality,
                    is as pitiful as if sunk in depression.
My mind, though wishing to flow, is sunk in a well,
and my body can't pull it free.
Oh! the depths of depression and the well.
Is depression that doesn't end
as deep as a well?
The gate is soaked by everyone's sorrow.
So are the scriptures and, finally, even words I want to say.
When I linger near the meditation hall of Master Iru—
my school friend who entered dauntlessly—
I'm greeted by the honeysuckle's white smile,
and unable to hide any longer,
I collapse beneath a withered tree.
Peering at rotting leaves turning to mulch
before examining my life
and the darkness of its scars, discarding all,
looking for a place to live,
pulled into solitude, into wisdom,
I would have walked the path to the other world.

---

1. A novel by Mochtar Llubis (b. 1919), translated by Claire Holt. (Kuala Lumpar: Oxford University Press, 1983).

At Moments Like This, I Always Blush

How beautiful the pair of birds in the autumn sky.
Their beauty and perfection surpass any poem of mine.
I couldn't write the world that exists in small things.
I didn't see the poignant secrets within.
What trembles, what had been a tree, water, silent wind,
sound of water, sound of grass, even the road
I followed, crunching along its edge,
had tinges of vibrant life I didn't see.
I was only concerned about the flowers.
I'd put the world in a flower and carry it around.
The meaning of a flower, its name, its seeds, so small and round.
But because small things are beautiful,
birds drop round seeds on the world,
and trees lower the birds' nests.
At moments like this, I always blush
and, like a fetus, curl up.

Crescent Moon

The moon hangs on a nettle tree

I hang on
Mother's breast.

Longing for a mountain home,
the crested ibis flies away

Pretending not to notice,
the world's daughters
flowed into Mother's dark scorched heart

Moon, Moon
heart worn out,
moon-haloed Mother
did not live even half a full moon

Every Morning in the Mirror

Every morning, I look in the mirror.
I look at myself in the mirror.
The mirror is like water.
I sink in water, swallow water.

In water with nothing to cling to,
I splash around.
No one knows what's in me
in water.
They won't understand
the furrow in my heart,
the swamp under my rib,
the bog inside my head,
and my grave.

I have a life to rewrite,
my life, misread by the world.
A drowned life,
a secretly buried life.
I was written before I read.

Long compositions
stolen by others,
titles of my life
mistaken by them.
My life too long buried alive.

Every morning, I look in the mirror.
I look at myself in the mirror,
I'll soon be re-illuminated. I'll shine,
mirror-bright.

To Single Women

I heard that when birds without feet get tired,
they rest on the wind. Rest!

I heard that if you eat lots of wild cherries
you'll have occasion to shed tears. Tears!

I heard that bees converse
with sound. Converse!

I heard that if you blow a bugle in the woods
the hunt will go well. Hunt!

I heard that orange stonecrop grows only
in a barren rocky place. Barren place!

I heard that upon seeing Goethe,
Napoleon said, "A real man has come." Real man!

I heard that tragedy rather than comedy
is true art. True!

I heard that Michelangelo
was single. Single!

I heard that birds without feet
die when they descend to land. Die!

Pain doesn't know how to age. The end.

Black Cove

The tavern's red lamp flickers as though it will choke and go out.
The water below the breakwall breaks all day.
Blame waterways that were changed countless times, or people,
but the road that bends toward the port extends to the village;
no one can go back down that road.
Now is when the sound of water deepens.
Some nights, hearing a dog barking somewhere,
doglike life, I want to cry like a dog.
Is someone pushing the world out?
Do the flowers circling the flowerbed want to bloom again
        somewhere else?
When I look back, I've spent a whole day to this place,
passing the house of touch-me-nots, house of *panga* flowers,
        house dandelions,
passing the house of torment flowers, house of tear blossom...
even on flowers, scars. . . .
A scar is indeed a flower.
Pungent florid colors spread throughout the neighborhood,
a flock of floating clouds hovering inside.
Perhaps tomorrow it will rain;
part of the sky is completely black.

AK

Kang Ûngyo
(b. 1945)

Why I Write

Somewhere, a dog barks. The barking passes the cloudy sky, passes the trembling cherry blossoms, the poor roofs trembling next to the cherry blossoms, the shabby walls and walls lowering their heads against the shadow of the cherry blossoms, the windows looking out to the new dawn's green world, the pieces of cement lying every which way and still unable to open their eyes on the narrow dirt road, past blanket after blanket soaked in the salt of sweat, past golden pillows and pillows wet from last night's dream, past and past..., it comes running to me.

It Speaks

Make the unseen visible.
Make the visible unseen.
Make the unheard be heard.
The heard inaudible.

With your words.
Poetry, literature,
today's literature hills, all.

—from the epilogue to the collection *Day on a Star*

Rotation 1

Day wanes.
Faraway, an empty field falls,
winds of endless heavens, fold by fold—
someone sways alone
in a house on the road where waves crash—
Sunlight alone remains to the end
drags the city where? I don't know.

Day wanes.
Each day in our country
beautiful women fall, pile up,
walk fast, even in dreams.
The sand scattered beyond the bed
is endless, and no one can hide her flesh
facing dark centuries of life and death
that peel away fold by fold.

The house whimpers.
Day wanes.
Trapped by wind
an entire life trembles like ready-to-fall fruit.
On each high roof, the noise
of heaven's wide clocks secretly hangs,
aah, beautiful women of sand
pile up in the wilderness.

Shattering, we
leave long shadows behind us.

Leaves of Grass

I know the wind
that will blow on that far off day.
I know which windowsill
snow and rain, that day, will cross.
Late at night, when I'm unable to sleep,,
I'll walk out of my skin and sit outside.
On that day, I know, I'll see you cry and leave.
Holding the yellow hemp washcloth,
you'll try and try to wipe the blood away,
aah, after gazing at the sunset sky
for a day or two you'll leave.
I know, even if
we don't lie again beneath the earth.

Becoming Water

If we became water and met,
all arid households would rejoice.
If we stood with tall trees
and flowed with the sound of rain,
flowed and flowed until evening
then laid down in a river growing deeper
and moistened the roots of dying trees,
aah, we could reach
the pristine and blushing sea.

But now when we meet
it's as fire.
Already a charred bone
stokes things burning in the world.

You, standing myriad miles away,
after the fire
let's meet as flowing water,
speak with the sound of fire going out.
When you come
come by the clear wide, humanless sky.

Woods

A tree trembles.
When a tree trembles
two trees tremble.
When two trees tremble
three trees tremble.

Like this like this.

The dream of a tree
is the dream of two trees.
The dream of two trees
is the dream of three.

A tree nods its head.
Beside it
two trees nod.
Beside them
three trees nod.

There's no one here.
Without anyone
trees shake
and nod.

Like this like this
together.

In the Fog

In the fog
there are men and women waiting
and men and women who've stopped waiting.

In the fog
are men and women waking
and men and women
who've just gone to sleep.

At last
men and women becoming islands.
At last
men and women becoming dancing water.

Aah.

In the fog
men and women who haven't met
and men and women already separated
like sage flowers

scatter their dream seeds
across the vast land.

Sleet

Sleet.
Not refreshing like rain.
Not even refreshing like snow.
Breaking, spinning.
Turning in air
it falls without a trace.
The roads I've been running down,
hearts, restless hearts,
rising, rising,
thrashing spirits;
there is no heaven—

Fog blows in the fog.
In front of darkness, darkness blows.
In that darkness, in that air
wandering drop of blood, wandering piece of flesh
thrown here.
Parting grieves
a parting here.

Sleet.
Not refreshing like rain.
Not even refreshing like snow.
You
in the dark world of heaven and earth
one day break into sleet coming down.
Briefly briefly blowing out a sigh grassflower you.

Rise, Grass

Rise, grass.
Rise, grass.
Gather all fertilizer on earth.
Cluster of clouds, gather all cloud stems
and with face scratched
by tenacious roots, shine.
Scatter on heaven and earth
your voice voice cry.

Winds that blow now
have all passed in your breath.
Dreams now dreamt
were all pent up in your body.
Even huge tidal waves
have grazed your leaves,
came touching your shadows.

Rise, grass.
Rise, grass.
If the world's breath pours down as rain,
drink the rainwater.
If it comes down like snow
gather an armful.
Falling grass,
go ahead, yoho yoho!
Shine.
Lying prostrate like the dead,
narrowing your eyes—grass!

Spider

—at Haein Monastery

What I throw out to the world
is a silver thread, that thin line I throw.
After throwing out your line, you crouch
cunningly in a corner.

All wings
stand next to tall trees
with narrowed eyes.
With narrowed eyes
you wait for the spot of flesh
that will come riding a shadow.

We are all
a spot of warm flesh
or a shadow.
Longingly, longingly,
we wait with longing.

Twilight Song

At twilight we come closest.
At twilight leaves get warmest.
At twilight houses on water burn with the warmest light.
Twilight walkers,
at twilight your mothers await you.
At twilight you hold the warmest letter.
At twilight you'll send the letter from the water's post office.
At twilight you'll fold even the shadows,
spread water's warmest blanket,
dragging the entire night
and your mother with you.

Woman Hanging Laundry

On a day when sunlight pours like barium, a woman is hanging laundry, the woman walks dangerously near the roof's edge, at times shaking out an undershirt and rubbing it against the air, from here it looks like the air and the woman are very close, the woman's life comes running and blows next to the blanket, the woman laughs, the woman's laughter crosses the air, crosses the sunlight and seeps into our flesh held inside the hamper, winds blowing here and there, equivocating clouds.

The woman hangs a child's one-piece outfit now. Like a dancer she raises her heels and, shaking it out against the air, hangs it on the line. A child's cry is heard far away. The woman's dance is done. She runs. Holding clouds.

AC

Mun Chônghûi
(b. 1947)

Why I Write

To me, poetry means passion, not purpose.

The permanent scenery of my poetry comes from the waves of a lone bird's wings that fly over the blue sky of my time.

First of all, I believe that poetry is the product of reality. But this doesn't necessarily mean that poetry should directly level criticism against the social order or the ruling class or reveal any intent to reform reality.

Although it sounds too fundamental or abrupt, the reason I say that poetry is the product of reality is closely related to the ordeals of today's reality wherein I live.

We live in a society where values are lost and minds corrupted, embracing a burden of lethargic intelligence more severely than during any other period.

Moreover, the material for literature is a live language, but the very language of this nation in this period has already been polluted and changed and has lost its original reality.

How vain it would be for a poet to sing of unreliable feelings or ideas using language that lacks reality in this high-speed era of overflowing information that enervates the print medium.

No matter how well this "world of vocabulary," the group of such words, is decorated with fancy expressions, it can never be called art or, even worse, poetry.

In the beginning I stated that poetry means passion to me, not purpose. I'd like to add that to me poetry is a matter of health, not a mere vocation.

My day begins with a frantic struggle to protect my health.

I don't know the outcome of this endless struggle. I know just one thing for sure.

I'll probably continue this sad, breathtaking struggle until the day I die.

The Storm

Isn't there a man
who will fasten his strong arms around my waist?

Like that wild Heathcliff with his untamed hair,
the unbearable sorrow

of a single-minded man
rolls around on the ground.

Roaring,
with disheveled hair,

oh, eerie yearning
that tears my throat,

from the distant wind
the grave runs toward me
to engulf my body.

On the dead mother's dining table
a bowl breaks by itself.

Following the flow of
a thousand sharp coughs

all night long, a woman resembling a silkworm
soars to the sky, to the sky.

The Stare

Don't misunderstand us
because of our silence.

Silent eyes are more fearful
than
flesh.

Becoming a summer bird,
struck by a sudden arrow,
collapsing into a pool of burning blood. . . .

We'll die, holding up the emperor of darkness,
who resides in the center of the sky;
indulging in setting fire,
our eyes won't die within.

The light in our eyes will bud
and become the light in the child's eyes
child's, child's.

The sparkling light
surrounding you
will stare at you till the end.

A Little Kitchen Song

The smell of fermenting wine
never leaves the kitchen,
the smell of a woman's
fading youth.
Her grief boils stew,
her love adds seasoning;
there's always
the crisp sound of scorching food
in the kitchen.
Two people standing under the same sky
since the day of creation;
one gives orders in the master bedroom,
the other, a permanent bed partner,
stands in the kitchen
like a one-eyed maid,
the sound of melted candle wax
pouring on her foot.
The acetic acid smell
of her blood fermenting in the kitchen
since who knows when. . . .
The cold sound of a witch's chopping board
grows loud and clear,
freeing her from heaven's punishment:
she was burned like a candle
to give light to the other.
Listen carefully:
the sound of a shy, young wife,
peeling off her skin, alone,
in our kitchen. . . .

Seeing Snow

Snow doesn't start its journey
from the sky,
it comes from a much farther place.

The place where we used to sway
before our birth in this world.

It comes from our hometown
where only empty swings hang.

It makes you greet
the first trail of flakes
splattering upon your hair—
a voice returning to life.

From the place,
free of our curiosity, our silence

Snow comes running
from such a far place
and finally becomes a glimmer of light.

The Letter

—To My Seventy-Eight-Year-Old Mother, Facing Death Alone at Home

Love only one,
give up everything else.

The one;
that's not life,
that's a promise.

Everyone leaves alone
but all head to the same place.
That's a joyful promise, Mother.

You came a little early
so you'll go a little early, too.

We came a little late,
so we'll go a little later.

We were born without promise
but keeping our promise in this life—
that's not a lonesome task.

Mother, please don't cry.
You were a beautiful fallen leaf.

To My Son

My son,
I guess there lives a god
between you and me.

Why do I get so anxious
when I call your name?
Why do I always pray
behind your back?

In your childhood,
there lived a tiny young god
between you and me.

Even a drop of love
could melt the whole universe.

My young love,
you've grown too tall in my eyes.

Who is this god
who lives between you and me
and lets this river endlessly flow?

Song of a Middle-Aged Woman

It's a strange season—
neither spring nor fall.

In perilously high-heeled pumps,
I walked around, puffed up.

Now it's the season that lets me see
half of the world
even in comfortable low-heeled shoes.

The season has finally come
that allows me to ignore elegant clothes and fancy ornaments,
to fling off heartbreaking yearning and pride,
to throw away my bra
and become indifferent to the wave of my breasts
and the eyes of onlookers.

The stifling season of gaining weight has come,
growing stories of children and arthritis
bigger than fruits,
redder than fallen leaves.

A Single Blossom

Where has the black flower seed gone
that was buried in the soil last year?

On the spot
instead of the seed, a single blossom.

Daylong
clang, clang,
rings a bell.

For the Sake of Man

As he becomes a father
begetting a daughter
a man bids good-bye to
that roaring beast inside him.
He finally learns God's passageway,
looking at the body of his daughter,
realizing the exit place is the same
for both God and baby,
he blushes suddenly.
When kissing his daughter,
he discovers his beard is a poisonous thorn.
A man makes peace with
that roaring beast inside him
as he becomes a father
to a daughter;
he becomes a beautiful man.

For the Sake of Man Again

Why is it so hard to meet a man these days?
The giant wave of a man's dashing body
floundering like young snake fish. . . .

Only a bunch of spiritless hybrids
always finishing up behind the back,
only a bundle of shabby hybrids
prowling in the shade.
It's hard to find a splendid wild horse.

Isn't the feminists' biggest mistake
to expel such thrilling loose fellows
from this world?
Is it easy to blame society?
Who pulled out their shiny teeth,
thinned their rough hair,
put shackles on their feet?

Too bad.
Every woman dreams of meeting
an unpolished wild man.
She wants to throw her life away
in the arms of a playboy, like a thirst.

Look at Antony, Caesar, and
Emperor Hsüan-tsung, destroyed by An Lushan.

That's not all! How about you, Napoleon,
even Don Juan and Pyôn Hakto?
How women love their insatiable appetites!

What's the matter? These days
there are plenty of petty men, dirty and shrewd,
who thrust their cowardly hands up under a skirt.

Those who wander the desert in search of flowers of fire,
singeing their dark eyebrows,
brilliant and confident,
they're an endangered species!

Antony: Mark Anthony (c. 82–30 B.C.), who ruled the eastern province of Rome, aligned himself with Cleopatra, the queen of Egypt, but was defeated by the forces of Octavian and committed suicide.

Emperor Hsüan-tsung: The seventh ruler of T'ang (712–754) whose reign is considered the high point of T'ang culture; also known for his undying love for his precious consort Yang.

An Lushan: A general of Sogdian descent and commander of the northern frontiers who revolted in 755 but was assassinated in 757.

Pyôn Hakto: An evil and lecherous governor of Namwôn who tortured Spring Frangrance for not serving him in *Song of Spring Frangrance*, a *p'ansori* narrative.

An Elderly Woman

—A Woman's Age

A woman begins to hide her age
at thirty.

No, starting at twenty-nine,
she gradually feels ashamed;
she lives her thirtieth year in shame,
like a thistle in the crack in a rock.

My friend,
you told me to greet the first birthday
that would truly free me from womanhood
and transform me into a human being,
on the day of my fortieth year, with a lit candle.
Consider this before you blow the candle out. You
won't become a true person that day.
Rather, you'll become an old hag,
no longer a woman,
no longer useful for anything.

A woman ages. Forty, then fifty.
The wide green pasture, already abandoned and in ruin,
only bandits in leather boots
are trampling through.

To You, My Beloved Ssuma Ch'ien

A song for a man (?145-86 B.C.) who suffered the humiliating punishment of castration for defending an imprisoned general who'd lost a battle, yet successfully proved "what humanity is" by writing the first large-scale history of China, *Records of the Grand Historian.*

All men in the world live
to raise a pillar.
A most powerful,
magnificent pillar,
capable of piercing age and night.

So they nibble on dog meat
and boiled penis of seal,
they rush about madly every day
and turn their eyes red
looking for wild ginseng.

Yet there's a man who's lived one thousand years
because his upright pillar was cut off.
There's a man who transformed into a real man
after being liberated from his pillar,

An arsonist who ignited a thousand-year history
with the flames in his eyes
that no pillar could put out.

All empty words
subside like an ebb;
only his voice remains alive.
Where Time swept by like sand,
there his huge footprints lie.

Here is a splendid man
who keeps a woman long awake
after a thousand years.   CK

91

Yi Kyŏngnim
(b. 1947)

Why I Write

Often I see things that should not be seen. It's been like that since child-hood, and I can't recall for certain what kind of events they are. I feel sure they're forbidden things, and this belief has led my life. The unknowable air that gathered behind my grandfather a few days before his death, the people who sit behind a wall of pink glass, a tall and hardy pine tree that sprang through the back of the mandarin fish my dad caught... As I grew up, I was often seized with an extravagant fantasy: if I walked a highway endlessly, there would be a bottomless abyss, bodies that jumped and plummeted headlong for centuries—a grand sight. When I woke up suddenly, the patchwork garden was filled with the sun's tiny children bowing obsequiously. I wish to write these things down, lock them in my notes.

At the Grave

Well, while wild roses grew around your head,
I walked through the market with pocket change.
While brambles large and small, grew near your hands and feet,
drunk on tear gas, I ran into alleys.
While you made a path through a thorny hollow,
I was lost in a windy city in unknowable things.
While you strained to push back invading acacia roots,
I saw my other self in flames, falling from the screen,
eating rice as though nothing were wrong.
While you cried "Cuckoo, cuckoo,"
mimicking a cuckoo in the forest around you
as if it were part of some secret symbology,
I panted, making love,
searched for the one who stole my money
until I had blisters on my feet.
I exchanged pleasantries with others,
longed for a man past his prime,
longed for him, longed for him.
While you hovered around a mountain,
filled with the fragrance of splendid wild roses,
each day I stood beneath the traffic light in the square
and sobbed.

Anam Street 1

Hope chewed and spit out, broken sleep,
something like spoiled longing
gathers under dim light in a shanty.
With no choice, I see your narrow shoulders
emerging from an alley.
When darkness sweeps the steep road,
the deserted path to the wealthy village
in the foothills is terribly white, oh life!
When a tall wind rises roughly uphill,
hunger assaults like a whirlwind of yellow sand!
A day is long as hunger,
and on the street unrealizable love piles up like waste—
I'd like to hide.
The sound of cold water seeps into a rocky hill,
sound of wind, harsh breathing, crying
and under them a mountain devoured by darkness.
Slowly its shadow grows.

Anam Street 2—Outside the Cinema

Each day the road splits into dozens of branches. Before me,
the dark road to Chegôn school at the foot of the hill.
At the community water supply, gaping water pails wait.
Charging the slope with a pail on my back,
I break stride and water leaps.
The path links and breaks like a whistle.
Wind escapes through the nineteen-hole briquet
furnace, mildew flowers, in full bloom,
a baby with dysentery's glassy eyes dies.
Sounds of rain carve space between graves,
tear at the paper in the screen.

Despair, like dried firewood, is aflame.
Crouching to warm myself,
it melts in my throat like a lie.
Each day, darkness falls, ankle-deep like snow.
I go to the cinema, following that dark road.
In the movie, on a wide, paved street
houses soar, brightly lit and tall,
and carefree people laugh and roll about.

Korean Women

I went to a psychiatrist to cure my anxiety.
The doctor, whose nameplate was encircled by two dragons, asked:
Are you getting on with your in-laws?
Do you have quarrels with your husband?
Are your children giving you a hard time?
No
No
No
Tilting his head, the doctor said:
Most Korean women suffer from one of these three.
Think carefully, and you'll find the cause.
No matter how hard I pondered, the answer was no.

Today I wanted to sleep with another man.
Today I wanted to get drunk.
Today I wanted to strip myself and loiter
in sunlit streets.
Today I wished to loosen my hair, laugh uproariously,
and feel splendid agonies.

Which country's woman am I?

Oh Life

How good it would be
if we could say no despair, no shame, and just worry.
Smooth concern, dim concern,
how good it would be if concern became deep,
The sun, like worry, rises slowly
under a tree that, like worry, ages blankly.
I don't mind swallowing burning shame,
eating with my enemies on a yellow wooden bench
amid the clanking of our spoons.
Then, above my head,
the once-violent wind may pass,
shaking the shadows in the square;
clouds drooping like concern may tease me atop the tree—

All right,
don't say it's the end, the door's closed,
and I can only worry.
How good it would be if I could only worry,
warm like concern, moist like concern,
if I could pass a season at ease—
it would be good to see the shadows
of flickering things in the room of worries,
concern that swishes by like stray cats outside the gate
that you can pretend not to notice,
like small insects glittering in the grass.
It would be good to throb quietly.

That, too, is like concern.

Chirping

Sparrows tired of chirping alight on the sloping roof
and scan the horizon.
Standing erect, has a distant place entered eyes
small as grains of barleycorn?
Is the reflected world small as a barley grain?
On telephone poles smaller than a grain,
within the world large as a grain,
telephone poles, houses, roads—
are they lined up in a row?
Trees smaller than a barleycorn tremble
with shadows the size of a mustard seed;
an old man leaning against that shadow sells shelled oysters.
Slowly sparrows close their sleepy eyes,
the world large as a barleycorn closes with a bang.
It is deliriously quiet.
Some begin to chirp again—
the sound flows down every valley of the roof,
tracing a deviant crease,
worlds large as a barleycorn
flow with short quick paces, trembling.

Song

In the world are many roads I havn't walked, and I have pain.
Those roads wind around my body and stifle me.
When I open my eyes, strange roads flourish,
the world spins like a dizzy head,
so many things I've not tried—my eyes are blank. . . .
Lighted houses where stories are made secretly after sunset,
light that blossoms like buckwheat flowers,
the brothels with outlines brightly lit—-
they made my eyes go blind and my body ache.
Regardless of time, my joints hold up,
my throat swells,
I've many cryings to cry;
my throat swells—
I still have many things for which to cry.
On such days my body is a flame.

Certain Sickness, Deep Love

With my sick body I climb a mountain—
a forest path with dense branches of small cares.
Every step forward, the unrelated sound of crumbling bodies,
the forest is full of moans.
With a swooshing sound, a young bird rises, flapping wings.
Below, a certain pain becomes a river and bends away.

When pain is great, it becomes a river—
aaaaaaaaah
It becomes a word that leaps in the heart—
a faint sound.

What deep sickness shouts far off?
What deep moan chisels the shuddering mountain?
Love, carrying a sick body torn by branches,
oh deeply ill body that climbs the ridge,
until that big pain pushes up against the mountaintop,
you and I.

Time 5

Only after radiant adulterous sex could I see the world.
I could see the earth's particles, void's windpipe, pain's pore,
despair's wrinkles and hope's dark spots,
trees standing dimly against want,
wind they hid in their crooks,
thin veins on the back of leaves,
green flesh lifted by hands of leaves,
leaves carrying a mountain range on their backs,
plodding the darkening road in search of their faraway homes—
barely finding their clustered homes, an iron gate in a blind alley—
refuse with worms and horseflies that idly rots;
lapped by blue mist, a giant gate opens quietly.
Beyond the gate, mist-wrapped things remove their clothes.
How dazzling, those white bodies
(my lover's owner's world)
You bitch!
Inside me a ghost with a topknot
who sat cross-legged for five centuries
grabbed my hair and threw me at the night sky.
Each night, riding moonlight, I wandered,
my tresses covering the sky.
Undulating world between locks of hair—
in it I saw him opening every closed gate
all night long.

PL

101

Ko Chônghûi
(1948-1991)

Born in 1948 in Haenam, South Chôlla, Ko Chônghûi (or Ko Sôngae) made her literary debut in 1975 and graduated from the Korean Theological Seminary in 1979. She served as secretary of the Kwangju YMCA student division, the Christian Academy's publication section, where she began to understand the structural contradictions of Korean society and launched her active career as a social critic and feminist writer. She took up the subject of the May 1980 Kwangju Uprising in a series of poems, including the five-part narrative poem "Ritual to Call Back the Spirits of the Dead" (1980). She was a founding member of the feminist organization Alternative Culture in 1984 and contributed to the Korean women's liberation movement as editor of a feminist newspaper (*Yôsông sinmum*, May 1988 to July 1989). A prolific writer, she published ten volumes of poetry in twelve years and visited the Philippines and Thailand in 1990.

On July 8, 1991, after delivering a paper titled "Feminist Realism and the Revolution of Literary Style" at the monthly forum sponsored by Alternative Culture, she carried out her lifelong wish to climb Mount Chiri, a source of inspiration for her poetry. The following day, she lost her footing at Paemsa Creek and drowned. Her funeral was held on June 11, 1991 in the front yard of the Kwangju Christian Hospital in Haenam.

Nôûi ch'immuge memarun naûi ipsul (My Parched Lips Upon Your Silence, 1993) is an anthology of Ko's selected letters, poems on the feminist movement, essays on feminist literature, and essays by friends paying tribute to her memory.

Our Baby is a Living Prayer

This world of day and night
is coupled as heaven and earth.
Heaven and earth become one body.
Raising grains, trees, and wild grass,
they live as a vow to continue life.

A baby is born
in the vow of heaven and earth.
What will the baby become once grown up?
A daughter will grow up to be a young woman,
then she will later become a mother.
A son will grow up to be a young man,
then he will later become a father.
A person becomes a father or mother
but man and woman become one body
and live with a desire for their longing to be inherited.

Look!
The future babies are conceived in the womb of affection.
What will they become once grown?
Our baby is a living prayer.
Baby girls and baby boys!
If our baby is asked to become the sun,
she will soar like the sun.
If asked to become a star,
she will shine like a star.
If our baby is asked to become hope,
she will rise like hope.
But if our baby is asked to become a tyrant,
she will become a tyrant.
If asked to become a doll, a doll she will be.
If asked to become despair, then she will be despair. Oh,
our baby is a living prayer.

If asked to become a road, then a road the baby will be,
If asked to become a prison, then a prison it will be,
If asked to become a plaything, then a plaything it will be.
Until then, you fast-growing babies!
But,
in a world where man and woman walk together,
everybody born
is owner of the universe.
Everybody can live
as owner of this land.

Prague Spring 6

——Lamenting the Twelve Generations

Mother,
perhaps you cannot stay asleep any longer.
Standing in a muddy, stump-filled court
with lonely wrinkles,
Mother.
You've been trampled down for more than two thousand years.
Biting your ten bloody fingers,
you still cannot give up on
the day of repentance.
Aren't you tired of your life of prison and slavery?
Selling your body to feed the little ones,
wandering the streets of international prostitution,
needles poking the six thousand joints of your body,
all the days of endless patience.
Selling your body to feed the little ones,
who have you been awaiting for so long?
The children of expectations are in and out of prison,
the children you cared for became homeless ghosts,
floating in the underworld,
but you still cannot give up on
the day of worshiping heaven and loving people.

Mother,
are you sure that day will come?
Do you believe
your hundred-day fast will work?
Today is your sixtieth anniversary in the twelfth generation.
The remaining descendants sit in groups,
with an unprecedented feast of words,
with an unprecedented feast of empty promises,
holding a big feast,
wishing you a life of many years.
Hiding the hunger cut deep into your heart,
flutter flutter, being dazed,
Mother.

Prague Spring 8

Oh, my, here comes a crazy wench.
Here comes the dazed crazy wench of May.
Here comes a lonely, lonely, crazy wench.
Here comes a crazy wench with wild hair.
Here comes a crazy wench with her breasts cut off.
Here comes a crazy wench soaked in tears and blood.
A crazy wench with a torn coat string,
a crazy wench being stoned from four corners,
a crazy wench with arms and legs scraped by stones,
here comes a crazy wench who lost her gall bladder and kidneys.

Oh, oh, here comes a crazy wench of May.
Hee, hee, the crazy wench poking at God,
stabbing a knife into the artery of heaven.
Here comes a crazy wench who doesn't believe in tomorrow,
a crazy wench who's absolutely, completely forgotten,
Whose death certificate is already issued.
Here comes a crazy wench with flaming eyes,
a crazy wench who bleeds uncontrolably,
a barefoot crazy wench unafraid of anything,
here comes a crazy wench holding nothing back.

"Who will get attacked?"
With mad energy swelling in her limbs,
with a torch in one hand,
with a Korean sickle in another,
racing with thousands of ghosts,
wishing to burn trash,
wishing to cut down the idiots' weeds,
oh, the scary lunatic.
Here comes a dangerous, crazy wench.
(Yôôngja, Suunja. . . . Here comes a crazy wench.
Check the door. . . . .xx[1] is best at a time like this.)

1. The original has xx, perhaps a word censored.

Let's Open the Dam

—To "Literature of Women's Liberation"

Let's open the dam,
flapping and waving our skirts.
Let's open the dam,
tying one coat string to another.
Let's open the dam now
that used to caress the grandmother's labor
and wash the mother's plow.
Let's open the dam of three mute years.
Let's open the dam of three deaf years.
Let's open the dam of three blind years.
Let's let out water showered with moonlight.
A grandmother is not rice.
A mother is not rice cake.
A woman for a man, a man for a woman,
let's let out enough water to cover the peninsula
and restore dry paddy fields scorched for nine years,
wet parched hills and waters of seven times three years.
Friend of long, lonely darkness,
the water has circled desolate streets of dreams.
Let's break down wayward barriers
and climb over despotic icebergs
by opening the overflowing dam.
The rocky cliff destroying this land of five thousand years,
let's set a tunneler to work on the base rock of oppression
and let the dynamite of love explode
and let huge light cover a water vein.
A hundred faces are better than one,
a thousand faces better than a hundred.
 Sisters, brothers,
let's finally open the sluice gate of freedom for each other
and open a waterway leading to the Yellow River.
Then *kugugugu kugugugu*,
let a flock of doves come and cover the sky.
Honking and honking,
let a flock of seagulls come and cover the horizon.

107

A Study of Women's History 4

—The Beaten God

A skinny woman is beaten under the eaves
by a drunk.
Her locks disheveled, clothes torn,
tumbling like a whirlwind,
stuck in a mud hole of conspiracy,
hit in the ribs by a tear-gas bomb of hatred.
Facing the moonlight helplessly,
like an animal, like a slave,
she is being beaten by a club.

A mother inside the woman is beaten.
A father inside the woman is beaten and falls.
Brothers and sisters inside the woman are beaten, bleed, and fall.
A grandmother inside the woman is beaten, bleeds and falls, thrusting a
        dagger.
God inside the woman
is beaten, bleeds and falls, thrusting a dagger, then dies with a moan.
The root of a nation inside the woman
is beaten, bleeds and falls, thrusting a dagger, then dies with a moan.

In the deep of night a man falls asleep under a blanket of violence;
the world follows him in and sleeps.
The virus of wrath blooming like a flower
in the woman's soul, filled with the lasting regret of summer frost,
drowns all the peace on this earth
in rainbow colors.
Ah, ah, it's scorching heaven's seeds.

A Study of Women's History 6

—A Woman of Crisis

There were days when the Korean checkerboard was set
     in a woman's way
but the game was played by a man's rule.
There were days when seeds were sown in a woman's way
but the harvesting was done by a man's rule.
There were days when a plant took root in a woman's way,
but its flowers bloomed by a man's rule.
With man's rule over woman's way,
the big gate was bolted
and the branch arching over the wall was cut.
Such perfect peace,
perfect happiness.
But one day
those days of love dreamed in a woman's way
and lived by a man's rule
spilled on the graceful table of the middle-aged.
A dark and fearful premonition
where ghosts with wild hair enjoyed a feast
and the fruits of love laid down in a grave
below the coffin of the bloody moon.
The shadow of twilight flickering far away,
the measure of the earth shaking in solitude. . . .

The riverside echoes with, "Why, why do you live?"
The boat watched by a solitary woman begins to float.

People of the Earth 8

—Mother, My Mother

When I can't face myself,
I softly whisper—Mother.
Turning away from gangrenous loneliness,
I call the name at dawn—Mother.
Mother who coolly filters warm blood,
Mother more indifferent than the light of the moon.

When I can't control myself,
I open the northern window and whisper—Mother.
Each sunrise I call her name—Mother.
Mother, like leaves of acacia,
Mother, last banner of this world,
Mother, hands like the beginning, like the end.

When waves of moonlight fill the world,
I call out toward a yellow field—Mother.
Mother, covering the calamity of the world,
Mother, forever filling heaven and earth,
Oh, Mother, who gave birth to God.

What is History? 1

—The Snake and the Woman

The bars of Kangnam¹ were dark, damp, and desolate.
Midnight people with "stamina" written on their faces
moaned like dogs in heat.
In the darkness of a desolate land,
a woman took a thread off her naked body.
The Kangnam district copied her and stripped.

Over the woman's swollen breasts,
over the dimly shining nude of Kangnam,
proudly,
a snake resembling the penis of a horse, slithered up.
With glittering goose bumps,
and stiff as a penis
although it was a snake,
it caressed the woman's breasts,
wound around the neck of Kangnam and swayed,
darted a tongue inside the woman's mouth,
climbed down the back of Kangnam,
arrived at the woman's private bush,
the paradise of the world's beginning,
and, ruthless as a dictator, stuck its head
into the beautiful womb of Kangnam.
The woman screamed quietly,
and the lights of Kangnam all went out at once.

In the desolate wasteland of a grave,
a skeleton man whispered shamelessly.

"A snake is a penis.
Eve was seduced by the first penis."

In the wine glasses of skeletons cheering with laughter,
a snake's semem overflowed.

Pestilence prevailed everywhere.
The vampire of Kangnam quietly smiled.

Now this self-indulgent place needs sword and spear.
A sword of freedom to slice off
the snake's intrusive head,
a spear of freedom thrust into
the vampire's white and shining mouth.

1. Area south of the Han River in Seoul, known for its amusement parks.

On the Way to Ch'ŏngju

—To Han Chônga

On the way to Ch'ŏngju
in an field empty after autumn gathering,
I ran, by chance, into vast silence.
On each furrow filled with harvest's pain,
mindless wildflowers waved, as in a painting.
Along the footpath of the silent field,
autumn sunlight warmly
embraced a poplar tree's ideals.
Autumn sunlight warmed
the orchard and a desolate path,
and made a fire next to a brook.
Autumn sunlight warmed
the village, roofs, and windows,
putting a wild wind to sleep.
Autumn sunlight warmed
sunny spots on hills and slopes.
"Don't worry, don't worry," it said
as it caressed shabby scrub trees.

Oh, friend who came with me all the way to the end
in such tremendous silence.
Today, frost covered my mind
and fallen leaves piled up here and there.
Friend, like sunlight, like fire,
your radiance becomes a warm blanket
covering the idea of our life together,
your flame becomes warm lamplight
illuminating the road we walk.

Sisters, Now We Are the Path and the Light
            —On the First Anniversary of the Womens' Newspaper

Sisters,
now we are the path and the light.
Now we are the rice and the hope.
When twenty million women lit the fire of heart's desire,
trust stacked on the wishes of one hundred people,
floating a full moon on the river of one thousand people,
half of heaven returned,
half of earth returned,
half of humanity returned,
and on that day a new world history began.
When you wakened the river of silence sleeping in you,
pulled out the nail of oppression buried in you,
cut down the weeds of discrimination
grown dense within,
and polished the path we were to travel,
ah, in a storm stained with suffering,
we saw clearly what we were meant to see,
heard directly what we were meant to hear,
spoke properly what we were meant to say,
and built a free-speech bridge.
At last,
the other half's monopoly began to crumble.
At last,
the other half's cultural monopoly doused its flame.
At last,
the other half's monopoly on happiness collapsed.
Three hundred sixty-five days in a year,
fifty-four lamps get lighted,
a flame soars in the hearts of twenty million.
At last in the Korean peninsula we pray
for women's wind, new wind, and the vigor of heaven and earth.
The flames that spread from one to two,
from one million to ten million to a hundred million,

all gather here.
This flame is the flame of equality.
This energy is the energy of unification.
This wind is the wind of freedom.
Sisters,
now we are the path and the light.
Now we are the rice and the hope.
Now we are the love and the home.

It Will Be a New World

Men gathered and came up with domination,
domination gathered and brought about war,
war continued and created oppression.

What will it be if women unite?
If women unite, they'll bring love.

All women give birth to life.
All life brings freedom.
All freedom brings liberation.
All liberation brings peace.
All peace brings homes.
All homes bring equality.
All equality brings happiness.

What will it be if women unite?
It will be a new world.

A Letter Written With the Left Hand

On the way home after seeing you,
I always cry as I near Anyang.
While I enjoy your lingering image,
examining it again and again,
I see your solitary independence and the coldness
no one can approach
clearly drawn on your shoulders as you turn.
Your loneliness and coldness
fall on my warm heart
like snowflakes
as I approach Anyang.

Facing your solitary independence and coldness,
I feel deep sorrow on the way back home.
I've traveled too far to go back;
I've planted too much in your land
to move ahead.
Where in that darkness lonely as a craggy mountain
can my seeds put forth blooms?
Where in that appalling solitude
can the gentle spring breeze blow?

Tonight, the declining moon follows me home.
Caressing me, she says, "Don't worry, don't worry."
I just laugh as I open the door.
There's no snowflake that won't melt with tears!
No coldness that won't melt in fire!

CK

Ch'oe Sûngja
(b. 1952)

Why I Write

The question I hate most is, "What's poetry for?" It's just as meaningless to ask, "What's poetry not for?"

Poetry is not a separate existence, much less an existence for something else. Poetry just exists. If life is a point on a circle, poetry is where timelessness and timefulness meet on that circle of existence.

No one owns poetry. It's not mine or yours but is somewhere between us. It's always on its way from one point to another. Thus, I breathe in the air you exhaled some centuries ago and vice versa.

There's a red rose. And there's a mind that says, "How beautiful is the rose!" Then which is beautiful: the rose or the mind?

There are forms—some beautiful, some ugly, some happy, some sad. And there is the eye that sees them, saying, "Aha! There they are!" Then which would you call poetry: the forms or the eye?

Communication is at once the most superficial and the most profound creation. Here's a small stone—my poem. I pick it up and throw it straight to you across the ocean, hoping it will reach you and be returned to me.

My Phone Rings Endlessly

Many people have drifted away.
With desire and sorrow, the scraps of desire, on their backs,
they drifted away, passing my window.
I didn't drift away.

I didn't drift away.
Mixing desire and disillusionment
I produced a day,
produced a year,
and made my monthly payment to death on time.

Yes, my phone rings endlessly,
and I don't want to avoid it.
Even if I sink into a pit,
I want to touch you,
fate.

But I always shut the door and locked it,
shut and locked my eyes and ears.
I became a complete machine, reflexes conditioned
to call for rice in the morning,
to cram with sleep at night.

Helmsman of the sky, old nihilist
who runs the great machine of emptiness in the sky's vacant lot,
is it you or me?
Who will wear out first?
(Of course, I know the answer;
I created you.)

My phone rings endlessly
and at the end of the line, like a cave,
a rotten swamp, hangs your mouth.

From there one day Death
will decisively summon me
and I'll decisively answer.
The burning fuse of my fate
will explode in your rotten mouth,
completing the vanity of vanities
begun thirty years ago, in vain.

Old nihilist, you'll toss out a bloodied laugh
and with that old body begin to quietly
steer the machine of emptiness again
to show you've accomplished the vanity of all vanities
started thousands of years ago, in vain.

About Women

Every woman has a tomb in her body
where death and birth sweat;
all humans struggle to leave
this harbor, eternally blind.
Like the Altamira Caves, like the ruin of a great temple,
like a hard, dead sea, the women lie down.
Birds make their homes
inside of women. A sandstorm blows.
The shells of the eggs the birds hatched from
and the remains of death are piled like empty cartridges.
For something to be born and to die
it must pass the ruined temple and the hard, dead sea.

For the Second Time in Thirty-Three Years

For the second time in thirty-three years,
I'm determined to run away from myself.
First, I detach my head
and put it on the shelf.
I remove two arms, two legs,
and put them on the desk,
detach my torso and seat it on the chair.
I sneak out on my squeaking feet
and begin to desperately run.
Running and running
till I can't run anymore,
till I want to quietly rest.
Someone walks over there, in front of me.
I run to him and ask for sympathy.
Ask to rest a while in his arms,
and if possible to die in his arms,
lightly lightly, like air released from a balloon.
He walks away pretending he didn't hear.
I beg for sympathy again
and soon, reluctantly, as if annoyed,
he turns around to see me.

A crushed face
that is. . .
my own.

House of Memories

Turning those many lefts and rights,
I couldn't reach
the promised land.

Even that woman who used to sing, "Give me
that hand of hatred, petal of revenge,"
laid down long ago in the empty room
where wind and water leak,
and crumbled away to dust.

Then, what's this?
My fate, my dream?
Is fate another name for the dream we dream ourselves?

In the house of memories uneasy winds always creak,
in the house of memories the trivial
tallies of sorrow always overflow.

What must I inscribe on the days of my life,
what must I add and what must I subtract?

The wall shakes quietly when I look carefully,
and cracks when I look even closer,
revealing shadows of people who live inside
or the sounds of their deep sighs.

What must I add and what must I subtract?
Early on, I was one of them
and I'm one of them still, but
when I briefly close my eyes the wall closes again,
and the people are trapped inside.
Inside the wall is a wall, but I'm trapped, too.
Outside the wall is a wall.

The world that I see,
the dream the wall dreams.

From somewhere, darkness grows.
Hungry, longing eyes light up
in the window where
my lifelong dream
freezes like a faraway star
I want to reach again.

The land of the father,
that side of the river with quivering light.

From Early On I Was

From early on I was nothing.
Mold on dry bread,
stinking stain on the wall from years of piss,
thousand-year-old corpse still covered with maggots.

No parents raised me.
Sleeping in rat holes, eating the liver of fleas,
vacantly dying anywhere.
From early on I was nothing.

So don't say you know me when
we pass for a moment
like falling stars.
I don't know you I don't know you.
You, beloved, dear, happiness.
You, beloved, dear, love.

The fact that I'm alive
is nothing but an eternal rumor.

While Watching Sunset

That thirst for living day to day,
like intoxication, like being pickled in salt.
Pain spreading on someone's retina, like steam.
But even then it's not me, I can't.

Chôlla Province or Georgia
somewhere a painful sun sets again.

Look, look, look at that red sunset.
Someone is frantically dying instead of me
painting blood all over the windowpane.

With heart and soul the sun sets
with heart and soul someone dies
with heart and soul the earth spins, and when it spins,
I look out at the world from an incubator.

When you're finally dead, my job is only

to wear white gloves,
shine coolly,
and enter your death for the first time.

Instead of a Dream

Instead of a dream we want a definite hand.
Definite, materialistic hand.

In the justice of Arabia—the sword!
In the justice of America—the gun!
In the justice of Korea—a drink! Dri-nk?

But certainty is only our half-sleep and half-awareness,
in fog as taut as metal wire
dead helicopters float and
even if political power has changed
we no longer sing inside the grave.
Unexpected letters come from a faraway country,
and we return them unread.
Late at night we close the history book,
worrying about sleep, and
suddenly someone stomps his feet
inside the closed book, and
we fall asleep chanting a spell:

My lord, if you can,
pour this cup
down your throat.

Night Owl

A night owl peered at me
from the window.
I got flustered and closed all
my body's orifices but
the owl's eye scanned every inch
of my body, like a machine,
and fired yellow beams.
My four limbs dangling
and numb, I was slowly melting.

Finally sleep, the closed, steel-gray sea.
Shadow man who hides inside,
loiters dizzily in the back of my dream,
and flickers like an apparation in the window, who are you?
Pouring vague headache and pain on me, who are you?
Sunk low into the couch of my stillborn,
who are you? Who who who. . . ?

That night owl clawed all night, destroying my roof.
It was hazy in the morning,
and rain dripped into my open brain.
On my dead body
someone vigorously pissed,
then, whistling leisurely, left.

Portrait of the Marginalized

He learns the grammar of this world each time,
but each time he forgets.
Is the world anesthetized?
Is his brain anesthetized?
He can never make a judgment.
He knows well the passage where
matter changes to spirit, spirit to material
but at times, he's far too ignorant.

The marginalized, out of habit, fretfully awaits
the time for the newspaper's delivery,
the time when television broadcasts start.
The marginalized every now and then
calls 116 without an area code to check
if the only clock in his house is correct,
listening until the computerized voice finishes its sentence.

The marginalized mostly commutes by subway
or cross-country bus.
He sometimes risks his life
and rides the bullet train.
Envying the happy people
who believe in the idea of happiness,
longing for the taut surface tension of Seoul,
he infinitely craves, infinitely hates
being taken,
from place to place,
from suburb to suburb.
From margin to margin,
the marginalized roams the map without a home
and blindly rambles, crossing time.

Untitled 2

I.
After the dew fell silently last night
the front door creaked,
and death came, taking the milkman's route.

The dark of someone's eyes,
and a dangling dark hand
on the door knob.

At that moment, a great shadow
came over me like a Titan truck
and I heard
the dark sound of a towering pine falling,
the dark sound of a generation stretching.

2.
1983. I hear fate's gears unwind.
A small passenger train falls onto an endless track
1983, God was rash
and I was powerless.
Oh all this sweat-causing conspiracy! Horror!
I can't cope with
this world, its terror of bare flesh.
But this world
surges
toward the deep center of my eyes,
marching like a hundred million combat boots.

Close your eyes, a frightening time will soon come,
pouring everything out; like it was intestines or marrow,
throw up your generation's rotten food
in the sleep of reality, in the reality of sleep.
And sink deep, deep.

(Quietly creeping at the bottom of a generation,
I changed into a multiped bug.)

3.
This generation's cup of death
is already filled;
your portion isn't necessary.
So leave!
Come back soon!

(When you wake up suddenly in the middle of the night
look into your mirror.
There I, the disgrace of the 20th century,
am sending you the faint smile of disgrace.)

Ladies and gentlemen,
you who are dying to kill me,
today my death show is over
after ten years
of putting on the same heart.
Please come to this place.

4.
When autumn brings the first chrysanthemum bud,
Mother lets out the sigh
she held back all her life.
Moon's halo scatters, scatters away.
The living will still enjoy the day's food.
The living, who are happy, will make their second child,
and unable to explain, this world will lie down,
unable to explain, the roads of this world float in a void.

Riding the depth of the wave of experience,
the cracked house

totters when hit by moonlight.
Can you hear? The sound of a giant pissing brilliantly
on the whole world.

(Someone watches me furtively outside the wall;
surely, it's my other mind.)

5.
Mother walks in my head,
quietly circling all corners of the world,
Mother walks continuously toward earth's opposite side,
walking long, working long,
passing Neptune, passing Pluto,
walking inside my dream without rest.
Finally, one morning, Mother
will arrive at my gate.

And now, inside, the grave of day to day shines
toward the only possible light,
but a child hurries preparations for his own birth
in front of the gray window before dawn.

Outside the gate, he who came by the mountain path
waits for me in his carriage.

Far away, breaking through the horizon's trap,
a bloodied seagull escapes.

Do You Remember Ch'ôngp'a Street?

In winter you were tender.
While the white hand of snow stroked our dream,
we wandered beneath warm ground
enfolded like flower petals.

Spring came and you left.
Lilac bloomed like ghosts
and you didn't smile, even from so far away.
Your eyes often made a sound like cellophane being crumpled
and your voice pierced me like an iron skewer;
yes, I was pierced silently for a long time.

Even if I have to crawl like a worm with a pierced body,
I want to be where you are.
I want to steal your warm light
to be pierced once again for the last time
and infinitely slowly die.

Now while I wander the vacant field
like an abandoned shoe

Do you remember Ch'ôngp'a Street?

When we used to wander in a snow-covered dream,
enfolded like flower petals?

That winter, centuries ago.

A Voice

The voice hidden in midair,
that with shining eyes,
wandered, in hiding, for ten years,
once said "I love you"
by someone's pillow.

Now you stand in memory,
a skeleton washed clean.
Through the hollow sockets of your eyes
blow two streams of wind.

As the tune of the bone violin shatters,
water flows out like stars,
and even on the wind bow's single stroke,
calcic memory rings clear
and begins to sing alone.

> In my house above the sea
> A bedroom of white waves. . . .

MH

Kim Sûnghûi
(b. 1952)

Why I Write

What is poetry? I enjoy going to the drugstore. There are so many medications there. I especially enjoy standing in front of the pain relievers and looking at them for a long time. Looking at all of them, I realize once again there is so much pain in this world, and that suddenly astonishes me. Despite the invention of all those pain relievers, there remains human suffering that can never be anesthetized. I write poetry because I'm seeking something that can't be found in the largest of drugstores.

I write poetry because the world that is offered to me isn't sufficient in itself. The world of La Doxa, the world of institutions, the world of "rightness" in which what is expected is naturally believed in, and the world is one of "of course," agreeing without reflection—I write because I dislike such worlds. My writing is a rejection of the world of "rightness" and the world of "of course."

Cold eggs in the refrigerator. I see faces in those chilled eggs. It's because of those eggs, sadly crying that they're cold, wanting to get out and fly away, free, pounding on the walls every night, that I write. Someday those eggs will burst from their shells, break out of the refrigerator, and fly away, free, into the sky. This is my dream. And because I hang onto this dream, I write poetry. The cold forces that oppress the fragile eggs' dreams of liberation are all too realistic, institutional, and formidable. I write because the social, political, and conventional forces that repress the dreams of eggs cause me pain. One has to become an anarchist egg to seek freedom and peace.

Therefore, the hardest struggle in the world is the battle against oneself. We're so well-trained by the world. I feel indeed that it takes the purest and strongest untamed passion to unravel the bonds of "rightness." When I felt the burst of a bird taking flight and soaring from the brightly burning flames of wounds, I smiled. I hope my poems bring smiles and yet are a grave festival of darkness.

Life Within an Egg

I.
We dream, don't we,
that we can only become stronger:
for the sake of life,
we want to build an even more solid house,
an even safer shell.
If only we could be as sturdy
as a wall that stands firm
and will never know collapse;
we seek hope as certain
as a steel bridge
that will never be demolished,
though there is no hope.

And we also know
that like eggs
tossed into the universe,
you and I are like eggs,
abandoned,
floating aimlessly in darkness.
When the floodgates open
and water tumbles out unannounced,
a small bubble is thrust into it:
pain as great as in a dream.

A small white egg
rapidly boiled in hot water—
feathers will never hatch
from a boiled egg—
screams from a silence terrifyingly calm.
(The complete peace of white, boiled eggs
lying quietly nestled in straw.)
The scrambled egg that disintegrates
in the scorching frying pan,

trembling like a female saint:
in no dream will its pain
be relieved.

As though floating through the universe in a solitary room,
we spend our only life
inside a barren and lonely egg.
We're sad because it lacks roots, and because it lacks roots,
it's a white conclusion
after
nameless exertion.

All eggs will break
and be shattered mercilessly,
but mine is a room,
a room
in which a small candle resembling my face
burns quietly, shedding light.
My bright smile spreads quietly,
with lipstick
touched by tears.

2.
When I open the refrigerator door, there's a row of eggs,
obediently arrayed;
cold, white, pure:
no matter how hungry I might be,
I can't eat them easily.

When I was out and about, having taken a suburban train
with no destination in mind,
I saw a poor woman selling
yellow chicks by the dozen
in front of an elementary school.

The chicks seethed inside a cardboard box
and bubbled over its rim,
soft yellow things
(life at its center is so warm).
The image of those chicks, happy just to be alive,
was caught in my eyes and suddenly welled up as tears.
Here I've been reciting just how unhappy I am to be alive.

Does this mean that I've been waiting all this time to hatch?
Ah, how sad:
on the top shelf of the cold refrigerator,
what can an egg yolk and white
inside their shell possibly dream?
In the hospital where my father lies, felled by a stroke,
my brothers and sisters worry about the expense.
Are the egg white and yolk
carrying on such a discussion of despair?

Refrigerator of four seasons, in every season
if I open the white door quietly,
I can almost hear whispering among the frigid eggs.
Mommy, Mommy, please hold me in your arms and keep me warm!
Like eggs never held by their mother hen,
like those sold below the suggested retail price,
I, too, am without a passport.
As the temperature of hope gradually falls,
my despair becomes more tranquil and detached.

4.
Hush! Be quiet!
In that egg,
something incomplete breathes.

Look!

Sitting on a shelf in our humble kitchen,
housed in fragile shells,
the children of God
fidget
all night,
trying to pull nails from the cross.

Hush! Be quiet!
In that barren egg that's begun to crack open,
King Tongmyông, King Suro, Hyôkkôse, King T'arhae,[1]
the blood of God circulates.

Your face never even had a chance to exorcise bad luck.
Don't you want to chirp anew in the spring,
to tear up your shroud,
and walk out to welcome the city of God,
singing *cock-a-doodle-doo, cock-a-doodle-doo?*

1. Birth from an egg is a recurrent motif in Korean foundation myths. Tongmyông (37 B.C.–19 B.C.) is the founder of Koguryô; Suro (42–199), the founder of Karak; Pak Hyôkkôse (57 B.C.–4 A.D.), the founder of Silla; T'arhae (57–80), the third king of Silla.

Female Buddha

It's not because I loved a man
that I suffer like this.
It's not because I shared a moment of pleasure with a man
that I have such excruciating pain.
Oh, women!
Women, you who cry, torn apart, who sob and flail!
In this sacred white cave,
man is no more than an accident
of the utmost triviality.
Like beasts, beasts, we chew at our entire body
and scream;
it's like a Buddhist monk entering Jhapita, the sea of flames,
in order to save his soul.
It's like setting sparks to a great pyre inside a kiln
to fire the whitest porcelain.

I feel as if a young slaughterhouse butcher were endlessly pounding
the top of my skull with an ax.
Each time the blade hacks into my soft spot,
endless petals of white flame spark
and scatter.
The petals of a mandala.
The baptism of compassion.

If you…have sins,
burn them.
If you…have any karma left,
burn it.

Why is the sound of a woman screaming
any less beautiful than that of a Buddhist chanting?
Primal sounds, more intense than a Buddhist's chants,
thickly fill a room white as a coffin.

Desperate tentacles of suffering and misery
grab hold of tearing flesh and shake.
Losing my mind, as though in ecstasy,
I seem to hear the pealing
of a temple bell from a distant universe.

The sound of a baby's cry . . . the first cry of a newborn,
suddenly rings in the great void,
and a clot of blood, heroic as a prophet,
stands bravely in the midst of life.
Where do we come from and where do we go…?
White sleep completely fills me,
closing all the doors of my body tight.

Hello. You've reached 385-2053. I'm very sorry I can't take your call now. If you'll leave your name and a number where I can reach you, I'll contact you right away. Please start speaking after the beep. . . .

Hello? Ms. Kim? This is Kim Myôngsun of Munhak Sangsa. I'm calling about the postscript to "Lady in Waiting." The deadline was three days ago. . . . You must have gone out. Please get in touch with me as soon as possible!

Hello? Mr. Pak Sôkkyu? This is Kim Sûnghûi. Of course, I'm hard at work. I'm not working on anything else, just so I can do that. Yes, but can you please give me just one more week? Of course, I don't leave the desk, not by so much as an inch, like a piece of chewing gum stuck on a step in an underground walkway. Don't worry. I'm sorry. . . .

Big Sis, Sûnghûi. Uh, it's me, Suyôn. You're out again? That money you borrowed last time, you said you'd pay it back by the end of the month, but I haven't heard from you. I'm going to Europe in a few days . . . um, to the ski slopes to get away from the heat. If life is the sea, money is the bow of the boat, right? Give me a call when you come in!

Hello, I'm sorry I can't take your call now. . . No. Isn't this Mr. Ch'oe Seun? I'm so absent-minded, I answered with the answering-machine on. Is it true that "Blue Flowers Made of Rags" has come out? No, I'm not busy. I'll come right now. Somewhere near Insa-dong[1]. Peacemaking. . . four o'clock. . . .

Hello. Is this the Soksem Institute? I'm Haein's mother. Would you please tell Haein that her mom had to go out unexpectedly and that she should come home around six o'clock. . . . Yes. Yes. Thank you. . . . Hello? Is this the Ehwa Violin School? I'm Wang In's mother. Could you please tell Wang In that his mom had to go out unexpectedly and that he should meet his older sister and come home with her around six o'clock. . . .

I walk along Insa-dong, that eternal street.
Having penetrated a thousand years of time,
preserved by only enough force to hold them in one piece,
some small clay figurines excavated from old tombs
stare at me quietly from behind a window.

How strong did the cohesive power have to be
to keep them so intact,
even in the realm of death?

Do I have that much strength?
Do I have any of myself left?

Parts of me
briefly meet and creak and agitate.
My mouth is full of dust and more dust, the dust
of a faltering parade of disguises—
I've been endlessly postponed
(and have long since disappeared).
Only some things resembling me endlessly agitate,
perhaps playing, giving a performance.
Covering the city's roofs completely,
a sunset hanging
like a tub of spilled mercurochrome
attacks,
as if to cover me with the red medication,
dusk.

1. A winding street in the middle of Seoul, known for its antique shops.

Love Song for the Belly Button 1

Dear You, whoever you are, if you show me your belly button, I'll love you. A small circle caked with dirt, all wound up, your sad little belly button—just like mine—is filled with shameful sin and silly desires in every nook and cranny. Dear You, you who were expelled from the womb of darkness, who aimlessly commit sin and die. Oh, You.

We're equal in our belly buttons.
They're the scars of our birthdays, the name tags of orphans,
the gentle grass of our flesh;
the vermilion lips of the white skeleton painted with phosphate
bite first.
We are so equal in our belly buttons.

Dear You, whoever you are, if you haven't abandoned your belly button, I'll heartily forgive you. When I see, in the springtime, new shoots budding on barren branches, when I see the birds spring suddenly into the air, my belly button itches, as if with eczema. And now my belly button isn't in the past perfect tense, but is budding, as always, in the present path of my life. And Mother . . . Ah, Mother . . . when I say this, I recall a woman walking along the beach, weeping. Pursuing her sorrow, her love, and her despair, my belly button enters the womb at the beginning of time. Mother . . . Mother, my secret entry into compassion and damnation. . . . Our dear Mother. . . .

Floating Metonymy 5

(What Should I Call This?)

Even love, tears, don't seem real.
Something like love,
something like tears,
something like scars,
something like rage,
such things, semblances,
envelop the thing resembling me;
milling about
in sunlight,
like floating motes of dust,
we form something like a life.

All those like me are
something like an era,
something like a country,
something like an intellectual,
something like suffering,
something like a scream.
With neither despair nor optimism,
in near darkness,
in this tomb where I exist,
there is life resembling death.

I can neither live nor die
something like a mom,
something like a wife,
something like a child,
something like a professor,
something like a poet
something like an actor
somewhere, as on a silver screen.

"You, really, truly, what are you going
to hang onto? Huh? Tell me!
Really, don't you have to hang onto something?"
Pestered, I didn't hang myself on anything,
there was nothing I could hang on to,

nothing even to hang.
Broken, I—no, I led all those like me,
like a loan shark, a crook—
no, from an infinitely high place
I pushed them out into an infinite descent,
like the liberation of a ladder
tumbling down, the pieces scattering. . . .

Growing Pearl 1

In the deep of night, vacantly
watching Jessica's Mystery Theater
on TV as I recline,
a white ribbon of urgent words streams by:
"RH NEGATIVE BLOOD, TYPE B,
URGENTLY SOUGHT, CONTACT THE EMERGENCY ROOM,
SINCH'ON SEVERANCE HOSPITAL, 392-0161,
IMMEDIATELY."

I don't have RH negative blood.
Lying there, munching onion rings,
I'm watching TV.

Did someone call me?
The night filling the window
seems to be staring ino my face.
I turn my back.
I say once more to myself,
I am not RH ne-ga-tive so why. . . ?

Thus
the eighties came to a close,
and I, who never lost a drop of blood,
I, who never willingly gave a drop,
feel myself disappearing
again and again, like onion rings
in the depths of someone's throat.

Is it good to disappear like this?
Is it all right to be swallowed up like this?
I'm falling asleep, as if rocks are piling up inside of me
(if they reach my throat, I'll sink
and happily drown).

Oh, no. Shedding my shroudlike pajamas,
putting on shoes fast as the wind,
going out a door stained by darkness' tears,
I begin to run, green ever so green,
toward dawn and Sinch'on Severance Hospital,
even though
I don't have RH ne-ga-tive type B blood. . . .

Institutions

A child colors in his coloring book all day.
There are butterflies, flowers, clouds,
and a river.
The child is afraid to color outside the lines.

Who taught him this fear?
Where did he learn not to go outside the lines?
The butterflies, flowers, clouds, and river are all
trapped within the lines.

Mommy, Mommy! The color shouldn't go past the lines, should it?
Fear floods the child's tender eyes.
My child, gentle and graceful, colors all day,
staying inside the lines, as instructed in the front of the book.

If I weren't his mom,
I'd say:
The hell with lines! La. La la! Color right over them!
        Let butterflies, rivers, flowers and clouds explode.
They're alive. La. La la!
Beyond the lines, wriggling and rising, they bloom.
They defy. They violate. La. La la!

I've so despised institutions,
and yet "Mom" is an institution.
To think that I bind you with the very thing
that bound me!
I'm both woman and governor-general!
Death to Mom! La. La la!

Soaring

My laugh was an ancient, a very ancient laugh.
From the beginning of time, in chaos,
my laugher mixed happily with the confusion.
When the universe was split open by the very first wound,
when I was pushed to the edge of the world and dangled precariously,
my laughing began, laughter to cover that abyss.
I might have been laughing at all the darkness in this world.

My laughter might have been the pain and suffering
of leaves that are blown in the wind,
and it might have been the sound of the world's
low tides ebbing before an advancing high tide.

At a subway station on Fifth Avenue in New York,
I was waiting for the train.
A woman standing by me suddenly began to laugh.
It sounded like a congested wheezing full of phlegm,
it sounded like coughing.
The heavy fate of evening filling that underground cave
mixed with the cry of a tired life between fingers that covered her face:
it might have been an evil spirit overflowing with intense joy.

As the train, casting opaque light, approached,
she threw herself down, falling
on the rails, where she died laughing.
Her life ended by the weight of the train, she left
a pool of blood, a pile of bones, a white kerchief
holding a few strands of bloodsoaked hair.
Her laughter, right up to the end, rang in that underground cave,
dark and low.

I suddenly remembered:
Mothers with white kerchiefs on their heads
in Argentina's Plaza de Mayo.

1980, May, in Kwangju, the anonymous graves and the missing,
the innumerable banners following the coffin of Yi Hanyol;
brilliant banners seemed to sob, urging the living to follow.
Black tears of Africa, like diamonds.

Don't shoot my son! The empty-handed mothers of Chechen
using their bodies to block
invading enemy tanks.

And I suddenly burst out laughing.
Unstoppable laughter that echoed in my lungs, against my ribs,
a suffocating laughter that burst out, bending my arms and legs,
my shoulders and my waist.
Is my laughter, echoing in a New York subway station,
my dark response, my tribute to the darkness of the human race?

My laughter hangs over an ancient, wide place.
When there's little hope, tragic comedies
and comic tragedies occur every day.
When I think of the excuses made for loss, brutal deprivation,
and the missing,
I laugh at each low tide, I laugh.
I laugh and
I laugh.

Dark laughter, pressed against despair as dark as coal is black,
vomiting up a great canal of crows' wings.
My lungs, like all lungs of my generation, afflicted with black-lung
      disease, I laugh
beside the grimy statue of Admiral Yi Sunsin[1] at Kwanghwa Gate.

---

1. The great admiral (1545–1598) who defeated the Japanese navy during the Japanese invasion of 1592–1598.

Wailer

Not knowing what to do
but cry,
I've been employed to cry
by the world.
Even when a breeze blows
and tiny love flows beneath my feet,
shaking my small veins
like the jolt of an earthquake,
I only partake of their beauty
when I cry.

Aesop was a slave.
Perhaps the world is more visible through the eyes of a slave.
Photographic paper made of sorrow
is the paper most sensitive.
Perhaps that's what God, the Almighty, who made Aesop,
wanted us to know.

Not knowing what to do
but cry,
I have been employed to cry
by the world.
Don't ever tell me, please,
that it's immoral madness
to build a wall of tears around my unhappiness.

God, in the beginning, made an egg.
Paradise was in the egg
and the egg in paradise.
God left with a smile.
One day the egg broke
and the universe was created.
Such is the wound of creation:

the blood that flowed yesterday flows today;
the wound that aches today will ache tomorrow.
To print that map of wounds
I simply wail
and I'm employed by the world
only to cry.
The hired wailer
walks at the head of the funeral cortège
and leaves the grave site
last:
wallpaper hanger
in the last paradise.

Mother's Feet

Look, dear daughter,
Mother's feet are large, aren't they?
Like a door to the good earth,
like a beam beneath the roof,
Mother's feet are large.

Mother's feet are large,
large and wide like love,
but, dear daughter, did you notice?
Mother's feet turn inward more and more,
the muscles are all turned in
like a hunchback's hump,
a leper's nose,
or the twisted deformity
of bound feet.

Five toes inside my shoes,
or rather ten,
send out sparks like the fuse on dynamite,
crying from the pain
of being randomly stepped on, like people
in underdeveloped nations
who ail from flu all their lives.

Inside Mother's shoes
are tombs of unknown white stars
that have been lost in the universe,
mysterious wings of wild birds
locked up for life behind bars,
a few bunches of pale flowers, dried,
and, like artificial flowers,
hung up and forgotten.

Daughter, look.
Roads I wanted to travel,
roads I've never traveled,
and roads I can't forget
still live in my dreams tonight.
I must flatten the roads I wander in my dreams,
using irons large and small.

As you grow taller,
your shadow also grows.
The entrance to sorrow expands.

All daughters in the world have wings
with which to beat the air,
but no woman ever flies through the sky.
All mothers in the world are good,
yet no woman in the world
is happy. . . .

Between Saint and Witch

Mommy, Mommy!
Please be holy,
like good mothers in Korea's traditional folktales!
Well, no! More like Lady Sin Saimdang.[1]
Be a perfect mother like Lady Sin Saimdang
and give me
the milk of your maternal love,
unchanging and unceasing throughout my life.
In this tough world,
how can I . . . ? If Mommy were to . . . If Mommy were to. . . .

Honey, Honey!
Please be a saint!
Give me medicine as a nurse would, and like a prostitute
bring me flowers. Be a strong and solid homemaker,
and offer me
a living room where happiness lasts forever.
In this tough world,
how can I . . . ? If you, Dear, were to . . . If you, Dear, were to . . . .

Women are becoming framed pictures.
Like a painting in a frame,
they're silent and still;
like framed family mottos,
they're peaceful and dignified.

Women are quietly selling off their souls.
Beautified to make men dream,
pasted on matboard and framed,

1. Sin Saimdang (1504–1551), the mother of Yi I, a great Neo-Confucian philoso-
pher, was versed in classics and literatue and renowned for her filiality. She was also a
painter of landscapes, plants, and insects.

turned quietly into "Family harmony accomplishes all things,"
she hangs unnoticed on a wall of the inner room.

Could Mona Lisa's smile be a laugh?
Or does she, perhaps cry?
Is her smile forgiving?
Or has she been betrayed?
I have no way of knowing,
but I can feel the force of a terrifying volcano
pounding beneath her dark breast,
beneath her shadowlike dress.
A volcano hot as the kitchen of a witch,

that male fantasies can't make beautiful
or plug,
makes her eternal smile
terrifying and strange.

She's undefinable,
neither saint nor witch.
A great painting of an eternal tornado
can be neither framed nor conquered
as "just a mother,"
"just a wife."
Love, to a woman, is punishment.

But a woman punished
becomes a goddess through love.
She, herself, frames eternity,
and with the world as her backdrop,
stands tall.

Na Hyesôk's Complex[1]

Dear friend, I have a certain fear.
After a pleasant dinner,
I sit, pretty as a cat on a windowsill;
chamber music flows;
swelling darkness knocks at the window,
a mysterious wind persists.
Quietly, as if it were a balloon,
I puncture my body,
and feel the white needle of death.
Air silently leaks out,
as though nothing were amiss.
Simply, breath ceases,
and the masks of housewife
and granny
crumple and fall, like tissue, from the wall.
It is the hour of lightness.

Dear friend, there were such women.
They removed their masks and set them on a living room shelf
next to the family portrait;
closed the door on their nondescript lives,
on "Family Day," a half-holiday,
having nothing to do with you or me.
"Your mother was ahead of her time."
One cold winter day,
they crossed that bridge.

Women are supposed to be afraid to cross the street.
They're supposed to feel dizzy and terrified crossing a bridge.
They walk arm in arm with their fathers or husbands.
But there were women who crossed bridges alone
on cold winter days,
who left rooms filled with chamber music
where the masks of housewife and old grandma hang,

and crossed that bridge alone;
from the other side they tell us
lion and lioness are both felines,
the same species of beast.
Women with flower garlands
shining wildly in their hair
left the melancholy enlightenment of the lion's mane,
quietly saying,
"Your mother was ahead of her time."

Na Hyesôk died on the street.
She collapsed from her journeys
through primeval, virgin forests.
Like blue sparks flying from a welder's torch tip,
her eyes, as she fell, illuminated the dark.
Women don't have a house in the Three Worlds;[2]
a father's house,
a husband's house,
a son's house, yes—
but not a woman's house.

Dear friend, something tells me
Na Hyesôk was not buried properly. Even after death,
she roams the Ninth Heaven.[3]
She comes to me now
and remains in me, my heart her spirit tablet.
And I, following superstition,
secretly keep her spirit.

Why
must a woman
tear herself to pieces
to build her own house?
Like a black butterfly, like a white butterfly,

why must a woman
who builds her own house
always face a miserable death?

KR/SR

1. Na Hyesôk (1896–1949) was the first Korean woman artist to work in Western-style oil painting. Educated in Japan and Europe, she was also a gifted writer of short stories.
2. According to Buddhist cosmology, there are three worlds: the world of desire-driven beings, the world of beings with form, and the world of beings without form.
3. In ancient Asian tradition, heaven has nine layers. The Ninth Heaven, the highest of the heavens, is the most mysterious and perfect of the heavens, and is where books that have reached neither the eyes nor the ears of humanity are kept.

Kim Chôngnan
(b.1953)

Why I Write

You ask why I write poetry? I don't "write" poetry. I live poetry. For me, poetry doesn't mean representation but existence. I don't copy or configure reality; I invent it. Thus, I've no interest in "expression" at all. What I'm interested in is the "form of existence." A form reproduced from the inside. The form of a woman. Giving birth to a child of new discussion with a minimum of the inner flesh of discussion left after all the philosophy and ideology are broken into bits and the contaminated skin is peeled away. And learning to live again with that child. And inventing the house, the form in which that life will live. That is the ultimate objective of my poetry. A house that isn't static, a house that shakes endlessly and is born anew every moment, denying itself. A form that is overlapped, composed, broken down, then overlapped again.

I put the seven-colored veil of the goddess Isis over the hard face of Parmenides in the name of life. Parmenides will be perplexed: he's completely forgotten the sense of what's "unknown" in his haste to persecute "what doesn't exist" and justify "what exists." I still see clearly, even while wearing the capricious veil. I accomplish beyond existence as much as within existence.

I escaped from the hell of phenomenology. The numerous others who wail inside me—I, Eurydice, to save what doesn't exist—no longer wait for Orpheus. I know that I'm my own Eurydice and Orpheus. To not look back. Namely, to no longer hang onto the eye of consciousness. To think with all of my body. To perceive as a woman's body, which is nature, teaches.

I begin from where Rimbaud gave up writing poetry and left for Africa. Rimbaud boarded a drunken ship to find the unknown, but I board a wide-awake ship. Men can't meet the unknown with clear minds, but I meet it with my mind clear.

I enter the water. A far, faraway road. But I'm not at all afraid.

The Sea at Twenty-Four

You were so beautiful. I held my breath. You fell asleep and reached the land of winds. I heard fluttering wings. Your soul, the swaying face I could touch if I stretched out my hand. The sea swelled to your face. The sea at twenty-four.

The sea was mighty. I wanted to bow to every direction.
Rain, falling on earth, rain. Absentminded youth sat outside.

I'm twenty-four, I want to die.
I'm just twenty-four, I want to die.

The sea flowed over your face. Moonlight, starlight, twenty-four.

The wind blew whoosh. Then the sudden assault of death.
How beautiful! I wanted to bow down again and again.

During the day, even if I shuddered from awkwardness, I repressed it and in front of the students, I talked about writing and dreaming. Unable to bear it, I fasted all day long. I couldn't stand it. These countless words, teeth-grinding, hovering, rags we have created.

This absurd life. I'm stuck like a grain of rice at the edge of a bowl called the world. Please forgive me, oh world, oh rice. I do my best to reveal my outer self.

A woman reflected in the subway train window at night. The animal within howled. Right? Really? Is it you? And the tears that come like revelation. I stood trembling from a certain center that we cannot name.

I crawled toward her. Let's not fly yet. Crying, I begged her. You must become at least yourself, let's do that. You must not become my ghost.

The Woman I Carelessly Killed

I saw a woman, a certain woman, or the woman, or another woman
                    (Hidden)
Falling. I saw it clearly because I shot the poison needle
of grievance at her with my corrupt words.
It's because of you, bitch!
My rotten saliva splattered her.

She fell feebly. I saw the light in her eyes
tremble slightly. And I realized that I must say good-bye
to May breezes, the sweet, languid absence of an afternoon,
the sycamore on the way to school, a necklace of persimmon flowers . . .
and to pure wandering. . . .

That woman began to rot immediately. Who cares?
I babbled as I pleased. I'm sick of it!
I looked down on her. . . .

My heart trembled. Oh, no, how much
I love you. Crying, I approached her,
rotting under the poisoned juice of corrupt words.

A woman, a certain woman, or that woman, or another woman

I embraced her tightly; the odor of decay spread.
(Oh, no! I'll try to find a way to revive you.)

Veronica, A Double Life

(Upon seeing a French film, *Le double vie de Veronique*)

High, far, within the allotted density,
pulling the decisive thirst of possible
homogeneity in one breath. Look how purity is dangerous.

Snap, the thread of life finally breaks,
and the dead stir
in front, back, beside, above, and below existence, anywhere
their figures hover.

Sunlight flies all over, under them
all the flickering fantasies, full of hints
that pass by, touching a layer of our lives
too vividly; a subtle distortion, a very small
change in density, and suddenly life is dangerous.

The beauty or the brush . . . sweet, different taste, of life, bitter
with ghosts who are too persuasive.

Pure fluttering, death, absence as tender as a friend.

I just lift my head, sunlight, light fingers
grazing my almost empty body as if breaking
oh how subtle, unaware I become double, Veronica,
I, dead and different, multiple I, infinite, light. . . .

Poetry

—Tracing a Line of Escape

Many entrances. Open. Everywhere. But reaching nowhere. Wandering. Severed arrival. Pushed-out existence. Expanding anywhere. But imprisoned within.

Innumerable Ks. Surely K. Given signifiers. But at once K which is not. That which is not only K.

I search for the animals. Terribly many Ks. My absurd arrangement of time. Always too fast and too late so as not to get caught in your web of language finely splitting and multiplying close to absence.

I multiply existence. I am anyone who lives anywhere any way. No use throwing the net. I can't be caught.

I live as if almost on the verge of collapse, but how well do I resist?

Trembling life. Unfamiliar goose bumps sprouting on my flesh.
And grim daily life. My antithesis
eagerly approaches that incoherence.

Nothing has ended. There's nothing that has ended.
Then life . . . death making scant progress . . . again . . . slowly. . . .

A Phone Call From Immortality—From Agnes to Mr. Kundera

(Upon reading Milan Kundera's *Immortalité*)

(Phone rings. Night. Queer loneliness. Such nights exist even at the end of the twentieth century.)

Hello.
It's me.
Who?

(Silence. The margin of emptiness trembles mercilessly. Disquiet.)

Agnes. The woman you cast away into absence.
Agnes? My goodness! How's everything? Is it all right there?
Well, as usual. Nothing particular. I plan to return.
Return? Where?
To you.
To me? For what?

(Small light laughter. That hardly matters whether it's there or not.)

To live with you. (A giggle.) Even though you kicked me out.

(Click. The sound of hanging up the receiver. Dark silence. An impure sound that begins to creep up.)
(Rustling footsteps. Knock. Knock.)

Between May and June

(What is clear kills what's unclear in order to be clear. What is clear is a shameless imperialism built atop the corpse of the unclear. I cannot stand life that is the death of what is not life, except when it takes a stance of opening itself to others.)

Between May and June
is a river of hesitation
splashing waters of a shoal

Between this and the other world
(that can be crossed!)
things begin to exist shyly bit by bit

Light green leaves
quiet, soft,
lovely awkwardness
hesitating tongue

"Now I've just started thinking about living.
What do you think? Is living worth it?"

I don't answer.
Anyway, once I or they are shoved in here
we have no room for choice.

Light-green leaves, shy
whether it's life or not
(I can bear that much).
Which will soon be certain to
become lively and self-evident then shameless.

Not yet occupied by an imperialism of being
the beauty of things still wet with the memory of totality

May—for a moment I endure life
finally June will come and life
will already be severely determined.

I gradually begin to die.

A Leafy Plant of Wisdom

Darkness or stillness. Essence, foundation. Soul, indescribable. A bridge between matter and form, and form and matter. Et cetera. At first, there is a dark low black clay wall, dark . . . really dark? Because the whole of this dark picture is illuminated by a rare method. Light comes from somewhere. Light . . . can only be supposed as a form of belief. The wall encircles the entire scene but is not blocked. It does not, however, mean that there is a hole in the wall. The hole cannot be seen but it opens clearly to a certain direction that cannot be confirmed.

That small leafy plant is being planted in dark soil inside the wall. It grows aslant, turns its body from the direction in which it was planted to another direction and continuously grows upward. The direction of its growth is particular. It falls sharply toward the earth then rises; falls again then rises. Thus, it grows tall bit by bit. At some time the fast-moving sharp top of the new sprout begins to emit bright light. It's not the light emitted by the new sprout itself, yet it gives the feeling that it's clearly illuminated by something. The illumination follows the new sprout's delicate shiver.

Ah! Meanwhile from the left corner appear two reliefs of babies' pale faces. The baby on the left has closed his eyes, while the baby on the right half-opens his. It looks like they're just waking up. Light comes from somewhere beyond the wall. That must be a form of belief.

Rain

From which heaven did you return
my bird of loneliness
the sound of building a house
between flesh and flesh
without pain

A woman weeping or not weeping, leaning her head
against the window of that house

She is like me or like my elder sister

A bird—lingering bird
with wet wings
like my elder sister
like myself
until dawn

The women behind us. Certain women. Women with light and deep, dark memory hung on their foreheads and eyes. I thought for a long time about those miserably beautiful and solitary women. About their tender, small bodies; and about what tears up their bodies and hangs them on hooks at the twelve corners of the world; what's cruel and beautiful; what has secret links with the world at a place unrelated to the world; what's still at the same place; what's awfully young, dangerous—about pure power. . . .

One low tree. A few modest, soft yellow-green leaves that, same as the winds, every time the winds blow, say; "I'm myself only within where I jump out of myself." Emaciated from yearning, becoming beautiful from yearning, having no moment to live because of purity's summons surging every moment, having no space to become a fixed existence in its life—the color yellow-green—the color of existence that only begins every day. I heard those leaves whisper, "I'm sleepy."

Dawn? . . . Afternoon? Between the not-yet-world and the world. Between the world and the not-yet-world. The women have come. Women without faces. Women with black clothes and white hats pulled down low. Whispering low, they surrounded the tree. Three, four? Ten, twelve? Through the yellow-green leaves, the low sun, drained of the toxicity of clearness, the dim sun that abandoned its conviction, shook.

The women were holding babies. One each. I don't know if the babies were girls or boys. Babies with the same vacant faces. In the women's eyeless sockets, tears welled up. And the tears began to flow toward the rivers of the world.

Women's Language

I say serenity. I already knew that words pulled me here but didn't truly understand. Now I can see language clearly from its head to its feet. Which ghosts enter my body and burn the midnight oil? I've never once worried that they might become ideas. What do you mean by that? To me, words are crawling babies who are always just being born, who have never lived, bumping their heads in every direction because they can't find the exit of meaning. They're so soft. The laughter of tumbling children can always be heard inside of me. They don't get hurt even if they fall, and it's fun. Do you want to see their home? It's open to outside, closed to inside. Because it's accomplished. ("Outside" is always a problem because they must come out. In other words, they must live. I'm sick of dignified and serious fathers meddling with a yardstick night and day!) But the door closed to outside is infinitely open to inside. (It might be better to call it the interior; this time, depth and quality are in question.) What do you mean the babies are obvious? I don't know. Don't you see the angel wings the babies are sitting on?

I say serenity. The dim bedroom of words. Angel dust flies about. And it smells of a five-hundred-year-old library. That place is nothing. I repeat, that place is nothing. That place, I say, is neither sad nor joyful nor cold nor hot nor wet nor dry. That place is just that place. Value, or some such thing, was created by fathers to live outside. I say serenity. I wouldn't speak if it weren't to live within language. I've never doubted that. That belief has sustained me to here.

To here. To here, where life trips over life and falls. But to here, where I've learned to stand so resiliently.

Images

—A Woman Who Went Outside, the Love of Fin-de-Siècle

Scene 1. Front angle, dark sky, or the middle of the universe. At first a seed of fire that appears like a dot. It starts to grow larger and turns left quickly. A tail of fire flying and whirling vigorously in all directions. The speed accelerates. Now, from the end of the flame appear faintly the words "god" and "love."

Scene 2. Inside the well. A deep, dark well seen from below, looking up. It's steep and high. Above the front wall of the well a narrow entrance can be seen. Sun glimmers around the entrance. The well is still dim. The moisture on the wall glitters, at times, in the light. Glimmering sunlight suddenly, radiantly pours its light down to the bottom of the well.

Scene 3. The middle of the city. The same angle as in Scene 2. A wide street with a row of buildings. Dawn. In front, on both sides, stand two tall buildings, with similar but slightly different colors and shapes. A gigantic black woman dripping blood appears between the two buildings. At first she staggers, but then she stands erect. When she's standing steadily, she stretches her hands slowly, arduously and embraces the two buildings. Sticky blood flows onto the surface of the walls. The sun rises slowly behind her head. Suddenly, she falls with the buildings in her arms. The buildings collapse with a roaring sound. Densely rising dust.

Scene 4. Again the front angle. The place where the city fell. Terrible ruins. Thick dust rises. The ruins' dim atmosphere and, contrarily, the brilliant clear sun. The sun moves slowly to the middle. When it has reached its zenith, a golden baby appears from where the woman fell. Dust slowly clears slowly, and the remnants of the ruins disappear. Small pointed light-green buds begin to sprout from the earth. From the baby's bosom, a small, poor church squeezes out.

PL

Yi Chinmyông
(b. 1955)

Why I Write

When the best of my life has disappeared, what should I do? Should I accept this life of excess as second best? Does poetry remain? Do only this single body and poetry uselessly remain? Why doesn't poetry leave me? Instead, on its knees, it looks up at me with constrained pleas. Perhaps the weakest of weak love. In this vast universe, this single body and poetry, the two became very, very tiny, and on their worn-out knees, faced each other solitarily for a long time. I wanted to throw it away. I did throw it away for many years. "No matter what happens, only you can control me at will." It speaks silently. Then, in this second-best life where the best light has disappeared, we pity each other; let me walk the path of the excess with it. Nodding my head, let me acknowledge it and say, "As I caress and take care of you, you there, like that." I could feel the word "love" blossom with a new name in a certain deep place within me. Since then, quivering tremulously, I clearly understand that I must and will write poetry.

Record of a Certain Summer

In summer, the house seemed ever so beautiful, timeless.
The house sat at the end of a road
in the part of town where I lived for a long while.
I liked to walk, so even in midsummer I'd climb the town road.
The house was the meanest in town
and in the most disrepair.
Its tiled roof was covered with plastic, weighed down with rocks.
Its door was old-fashioned, made of wood,
and the sky-blue paint had mostly peeled off.
The people in this house didn't seem to think to fix the tiles
or repaint the doors.
So that was how, out walking on a summer day, I first saw the house.
Compared to the width of the house, its backyard was really broad.
Even the imposing frames of new two-story houses
couldn't obscure that wide backyard.
Radishes, cabbages, lettuce, artichokes, spinach, green onions, peppers,
green things in labeled rows in the backyard, heavily tilled.
On tiptoe and tight to the wall, I could read the names all those things.
It was most likely the old one of the house.
The old one who took hoe and watering can, one in each hand,
to the garden, set down the watering can, and tilled the soil,
the old one who returned from the yard's other side, dragging the hose.
The old one never seemed to straighten her bent back,
so never saw me glued to the wall.
All that summer during my walks, I headed for that house
at the end of the road in the town.
But one side of the backyard opened to heaven.
To read the names of all the green things,
I spent days glued to the wall on tiptoe.
One day, the old one couldn't be seen.
I saw instead the empty watering can placed in the sunlight,
the hose pulled into the midst of the green things.
Lettuce, spinach, artichokes . . .
I kept on reading,

and I saw instead, placed, unnoticed, under the wall,
a mesh chair with the netting undone.
I saw instead a towel hanging from the back of the chair.
Summer sunlight in the backyard of that house, endless,
like images that pour down endlessly;
my face, above the wall all through that summer,
grew bright red as an apple.

Woman Mopping With a Rag Mop

I.
Long corridor.
The woman sitting on the floor at the corridor's end quietly rises.
She smoothes her wrinkled front.
She raises the handle of the mop in her lap.
She clutches the long handle and begins to push.
She continues to push,
whether she reaches the corridor's other side or not. Careworn.
The corridor is empty.
The closed door of every room holds its breath.
In the row of windows on one side of the hall,
setting sunlight floods in, claiming half of the corridor.
When I submerge myself
in the center of the sunlight, heat and power seep out.
Even through my worries, bits of peace and happiness visit me.
Peace and happiness like the scent of a mop.
Though this might be the way to the corridor's end,
the woman doesn't look at the windows, the closed doors of the rooms,
or toward the end of the corridor, on the other side.
She's not even looking at the spread and tangled mop.
She may reach the end of the corridor on the other side,
then return to the end of the corridor on this one,
but perhaps that woman,
before reaching the end on the other side,
anticipates the end on this side again,
that long handle clutched in her two hands
never swerves, pushing straight ahead.
She's never dropped that mop, not once.
She's never compared life on the corridor with anything.
When life on the lively corridor ends,
she'll wash the rag mop and place it, tidily, upright in its proper place
and end the work of this life.
She'll remove the bluish work dress and hang it on the white wall.
She'll rise at the corridor's end,

178

and disappear quietly through the back door.
Passed and pushed by the life of a dejected woman with a rag mop,
the entire corridor quietly shines.

Pure Talk

How quiet it is. The sound of the mouths of trees rubbing in the midst of the day. The slight coughs of the words falling on the edge of the yard. How high the world is. How dazzling to my eyes the sky is. Like the time I couldn't look straight at my lover descending a staircase. How red the edges of my eyelids are. Myriad forms float away; myriad forms float back. How quiet it is. Flowers that live only a year. How painful my back is. How painful my body is. The faded colors of grass-flowers called to the water's edge. People climbing a mountain will rest on a vacant stump. I'll fill up the sound echoing in every glass bottle. The dream of this life doesn't come with a single cigarette. I'll talk about the food supplies of the world. Myriad forms float away; myriad forms float back.

The Bear

The bear in the illustrated book of animals is fat and doesn't speak.
He sits resting his feet on a tree as big as his body.
He holds a fistful of vines he must have stripped off from somewhere.
The ripened fruits dangling from the vine are black like his eyes.
One paw is placed awkwardly on his head, as if feigning something.
When the bear meets a clump of rock, he butts against it, they say,
then steps back and butts it again, although that clump will never budge.
He probably went a bit of a distance and ran into a clump like that.
He must remember turning around, scratching the back of his head.
Near where the bear is seated, there is no chill in the autumn forest.
The tree leaves are a finely-colored brown, like the fur on his chest,
and the wide leaves that have fallen down, resemble his footprints.
When will he climb stealthily down the tree and slowly return to his den?
When the bluish evening air deepens,
and smoke rises from the village, entwines the vine tree, and hides the
        mountain peak,
the bear will probably lumber slowly to his den. After he arrives,
will he prepare for a sleep unknowable by those who haven't ripened,
black like his eyes?
The bear, leaning his body, still doesn't speak
and hasn't yet touched a single fruit on the vine.

Snow

It snowed. It snowed comfortably. No, that's not it. In the beginning, it snowed violently. Chill, freezing, biting cold. But when it came down in the evening, it snowed gently. It was warm. I called out "Snow." I heard the echo "Snow" follow me. Crystals of snow grass-flowers gathered. It snowed deep, deep. I sometimes held my breath beneath a lone lamp on the street. I'd floated from village to village and couldn't float anymore, so I was planning to freeze. It snowed. Today. White snow. No, it came down blue. But red. It also snowed red, like the blood vessel my mother burst. Thinking of last year's snow, I glued more grass-flowers on the windowpane. That high place. I heard the sound of a silver cane tapping. Tap. Tap. A picture in a child's storybook. You know, my mother went before me, became an angel and on snowy evenings, she comes back, walking with a silver cane. Tap. Tap. Ah, ah, come down, Mother. To this world, come down, walking with the silver cane. Mother made a path by waving the cane in quiet places. The path came nearer. When the path reached the naked branch at the very top of the tree, the tiny branches next to it shook. The path shook with them. The path, descending as it shook, became caught in the tangled branches, and there a distant wet fog arose. At last, that path flowed down, traveling on my two eyes. Ah, ah, her spirit, like lamplight, was hiding in my eyes. It snowed.

CS

Kim Hyesun
(b. 1955)

Why I Write

Why write poems? We write to love others. Our creator has hidden, inside and outside our bodies, infinite secrets of creation that we can discover only through loving others. So I write. In the act of writing poems, I love.

I dreamed. Of a single solitary virus that will enter my body and take over one of my cells. A virus that will enter this cell and use it as a host to swallow another. A virus that will in the end swallow my entire body. So small no one has noticed it yet. But someone, someday, will look at it through something like a microscope and cry out, intoxicated by its beauty.

I desire a single sentence like this virus. A single sentence whose structure will become the structure of the universe. One clause, one sentence, that will destroy, swallow up, the organization of my body. One sentence that will disappear with me.

One such "poor love machine" with which to fathom and pierce the world of chaos.

Where will this virus-like sentence come from? It will come from the ecological world of this broken power. With my vessel of imagery, I await the virus that will jump from the loop of this broken power. Like Ebola's monkey host, I lie in wait in the refuse heap of this ruined city, my entire body exposed, for that single solitary virus that can destroy you with a sentence of love.

Memories of the Day I Gave Birth to a Daughter
—In the Style of *P'ansori* Narrative

I enter through the open mirror
Inside the mirror sits Mother
I enter through the open mirror again
Inside this mirror sits Mother's mother
I push back the mirror where Grandmother sits
I cross the threshold
Inside the mirror sits smiling Great-grandmother
I thrust my head through Great-grandmother's smiling lips
Inside this mirror, Great-great-grandmother sits, her back to me
She is younger than I
I enter through the open mirror
Enter again
and again
The mirror darkens
Inside sit all the mothers of my ancestry
All these mothers swarm around me
mumbling "Mama, Mama"
rush toward me
chewing on their gums and wailing for my milk
But milk does not come
My insides are filled with air

My stomach grows larger than a balloon
It bobs aimlessly upon the sea
So vast is the mirror's interior
not a single straw can be grasped
Occasional lightning passes through my body
My body rushes headlong into the sea
All my mother's shoes at the bottom of the sea
are dissolving leisurely
A bolt from the blue
Power failure
Utter darkness

The mirrors collapse all at once
Shattering at my feet, they spew out one mother
People in white robes, their hands gloved,
clean away shards of glass and lift up
one tiny mother,
the mother of all mothers,
bloodstained and eyes closed,

and say, princess with ten fingers!

Not Knowing He's Dead

Not knowing he's dead
he hurries to his feet
knots a tie neatly
over the hollow chest
evenly applies oil
on the brittle hair
pours a cup of milk
into the maggot-infested entrails
slips shoes of cowhide
over the dead leather of his feet
and runs like the wind
through streets lined with tombstones

Not knowing he's dead
he returns, dusting himself off
spreads his bedding
beside the coffin of a dead woman
Brittle hair falls down in a pile
when he bends over
and cold teeth tumble out of his mouth
Wrinkled skin is shed
and drops on his feet

Not knowing he's dead
he enters death again
smacking his lips together with the fine phrase
to be engraved on his tombstone tomorrow
He lifts the coffin lid of his own accord.

Daybreak in Seoul

Daybreak, a van
rushes full speed into my sleep
eyeballs shatter loudly
and gingko leaves fall all at once
A woman gets out of the van first
There's a newborn on her back and a washcloth covering half her face
(The newborn on her back isn't her baby)
A man with a lopped-off rubber tire on each leg is next off the van
(Inside the bags of rubber tire, two handsome legs are folded up)
Next a one-armed child with sooty face
is released into an underpass farther on
with a child even smaller than he
(They're not brothers)
(Even in a dream world, recorded facts exist;
even in a dream world, I know all I need to know)
Beggars pour out of the van again and again
and fill the underpass
whining, panting, groping, crawling, flipping over
Believe in Jesus the kingdom of heaven is near
A gray-haired grandfather
takes out pictures of western babies
from a bundle under his arm
Prostrate yourself on the ground, make babies cry,
stretch out nonexistent legs, stir wounds
A blind couple passes, holding onto each other
They walk through a moving subway train
(They're not a couple)

Haven't I exhausted it in dreams
The picture repeats itself over and over
No wind blows and yet trees lining the streets crack
Before I can place a pair of disposable contacts on my shattered eyeballs
and wind the clock of a new work day
broken automatons descend into an underpass

Those who kicked off my blanket even before I did
open gaping mouths of baskets, not palms
and litter the lair of the hunger ghost
before dawn

National Museum Hallway

I notice my child is missing in the Choôon Dynasty Wing.

A rice bowl, wine cup, and spoon used by a king—I stop gazing at them like a forgotten royal consort. I run toward the Koryo Wing, brushing lotus petals off a white celadon ink pot. I run between jade-hued vases. They appear to be tilting and falling back. I run, my mind blank. A delicate crane leaps up, young pine and freshwater fish drop to the floor—I run. Running I call out her name softly. Kindling thrown into a fired-up kiln, the voice leaves no trace. I run out again. From Koryo to Silla, from Kaesông to Kyôngju, I run through doors I've kicked open, through a room tinkling with the jangling of gold earrings, jade earrings, glass earrings. My chest is frothing like gold being melted in aqua regia. What must I do? Did I just catch a glimpse of my child's head through the disinterred heaps of royal tombs? I thrust my hand between some articles of the tomb. T'ak! A pane of solid glass under the palm of my hand blocks me. I bolt from the Silla Wing to the Clay Pottery Age Wing. Please don't wander outside. It will be even harder to find you then. A clump of earth stands and becomes a vessel. A clump of earth stands and becomes a man. A clump of earth stands and becomes a water jar. All the vessels look like a child to me. A broken child put back together with glue. Over there stands a child filled with water. Hûijae Hûijae. I weep. Tears seep into the carpeted floor, and the postcards I bought at the museum's entrance scatter on the ground. At the entrance to the Stone Age Wing I call my child again. Smoke seems to rise from a stone stove. In spite of myself, I glance back once more. Hard to believe that animals were caught with swords, arrows, spears of stone. A roebuck flashes past and out the door. I stop chasing it and decide to look around the rest area. Its plush red drapes are magnificent. Is this a room where some ambassador to a foreign country was once commissioned? A piece of paper lowered to his head with the words, "Africa," or "Chile." Could the room have witnessed foreigners conferring on one another feathers of baronetage, earldom, dukedom, viscountcy? At noon, they'd spread their feathers and show off. Now Coca-Cola is sold here. I crash into someone and receive a baptism of Coca-Cola. Cola spreads like rotten blood on my white skirt. Whimpering, I go down the staircase. And come back up again. A labyrinth of squares. Suddenly I tumble into a room. Iron Age. A sword of iron. A shield of iron. A helmet of iron. I come out of the room again, turning my back on a spear made of iron. Just then, as though in a dream, I see my child coming up the staircase. Mom, what's this? Oh that, that's a suit of armor made of iron. To wear during a sword fight so that you won't be hit. It's probably heavy. In front of an iron soldier of the Iron Age, we grab each other's hands.

Taklamakan[1]

The woman washing her hair at sunrise
has no thighs.
She pours a bucketful of sand over her hair
and splash, dips her hair in a pool of sand.
The woman without feet
rinses her hair in a river of sand, swishing this way and that.
The woman without a chest.
The woman without hair.
Oh, the woman without even a body washes her hair.
We . . . neither come . . . nor go . . . you there . . .
I here
The brittle strands of crumbled days swell, straighten, ripple.
From sunrise to sundown,
without once straightening the back she does not have,
the woman washes her hair,
combing the waves in a river of sand.

1. A vast arid aerea in the Sinkiang-Uighur region of western China.

Inside the Iris

a shovelful or two of sand has been flung
into the vast sea under my eyelids
my eyelids have been closed
I'm left alone

in the sea
water flows
from the mountain's foot to the peak
as scaled birds soar
deep into the mountain
depth becomes height
high becomes low

there
when night falls
my dead grandmothers pass by
carefully lighting the lamps under our feet
clouds hover below us
people hang windows from the floor

fathers lay eggs in the wind
mothers raise the young between branches
there people erect a mountain range
reclaim land and scoop up a moon
deep is my vast ocean within this depth
a strange world in reverse

Women

did I write that I'll endure this
with sorrow for the road we didn't take
did I sentimentalize about . . . my beloved
or carry on about the brutal summer like a hypochondriac
did I ask what becomes of your birthdays when you're gone
couldn't I hide you in the folds of my skirt couldn't I do
as they do in the movies

will they come and bang on the gate
when the gate of every war is opened
women pour out
and block the gate of every war
shaking their heads
not here not here

couldn't I hide you in the folds of my skirt . . . a woman is shot she has
hidden a man in the folds of her skirt. A man swills a woman's blood she
has just taken her final breath. A woman rips out the inside of a couch
to prepare a place to hide him. A woman guts a piano to hide his bed.
This piano will remain mute even when the keys are struck. A woman
desperately straddles a large jar—she cries out: "He's not here, he's not
here, I didn't hide him." A woman chased to a shed lies on top of a man
she has hidden beneath the hay. "He's not here, he's not here, I didn't
hide him." They set the hay aflame.

after this after I die
how will my daughter remember me

a mother who tore out her entire forehead
to make a secret attic room
a mother who woke up in the middle of the night
and put on her glasses
unable to sleep for the weight of darkness
she mumbled in her sleep

he's not here he's not here I didn't hide him

an old woman without enough
strands left on her scalp to put a hairpin through
climbs a hill every evening,
leaning the weight of her body on a cane
she looks beyond the mouth of the village
and shakes her balding head side to side
he's not here he's not here I didn't hide him

with her large palm
she covers the fruit that the fig tree
without flowering has borne
she stands in the rain
shaking her head side to side

A Very Old Hotel

A very old hotel. A hotel that at night lies curled up like a cat by the river. There is a hotel like this. Within its breast there are rooms numbered 1992, 1993. . . . They tell me that you, my darling, lie sleeping in the room next to the one I've taken. The hotel is within my breast and I am in the hotel. In the hotel within my breast there's a bed covered with a blue blanket. I lie on that bed and the hotel lies within my breast. Outside the hotel within my breast a blue river flows like a pleat in wrinkled wool. A boat carrying tourists swells up to my head before ebbing away. Hung over, I gaze at this river. Or stand in front of windows that open only if I pull the handles toward me with all my might. The hotel breathes, pulsates. Soundless vacuum cleaners cross the red carpet of the hallways, a woman with a white hat shakes the dust off the hat and stretches her back. Keys to various rooms in the hotel within my breast are left at the front desk. I have a handful of invisible keys in my pocket but I can't open the doors and enter the rooms of this hotel within my breast. Ah, at night do lights come on in those rooms? When lights come on, I want to kick my blanket off and throw open the doors to the rooms of the hotel within my breast. My navel glows bright with this burning desire. When doors don't open, pull as I might, I want to call a strong person for help. A hotel that sometimes slinks along like a cat in the rain. A hotel that sometimes sweeps me up and hurls me out the window. They say that the I who's gone mad and stolen my sleep hides behind the wall clock at the end of the hallway. This hotel. When night, unlit, arrives, the hotel puts on a bewildered face, like a crown just excavated from a grave. The hotel appears unfamiliar even to me when I get up in the middle of the night. I open all the windows of my body and you stick your face out from under the hotel's shingles, from every line of the graph paper from which the roof is hung. When morning comes, the hotel flees like a nocturnal cat, hanging windows above the river again.

Mice

A scream that seems to be heard when we step into bright morning. Too deep to be heard by our ears. A scream let out by last night's darkness. This morning a white white scream out of the blue was scattered ah ah ah ah in the air and then gathered up. Do people know? How night's darkness suffers when you turn on the light! Night comes, but I can't turn on the light. The day of the first snow. Home after an MRI. Afterward I asked someone: Have you ever turned the light on in your insides? Was my essence the darkness of that limitless mass? With the light on inside my darkness, I shook my head to and fro like a pinned May beetle, poop poop poop. A black cord hung from my mouth. In a single breath I passed the reptilian stage and regressed into a May beetle. Struck by lightning, it lies on its back. Was my dignity, hidden in this black interior, none other than this darkness? When the light came on at once, my beloved Negro shivered inside my underground prison. Tonight the wounded walls of my room shudder as headlights seep in from outside. Hundreds of painful rays stab me as I sit curled up, my face black. The day of the first snow. Where has it all gone? White snow is nowhere to be seen and outside the window, houses are lighted. How night must suffer in that light.

A Teardrop

With a pair of tweezers he picks up a teardrop. My room is lifted, and my face with it. Sitting still, knees to my chest, I feel as though he's holding the room with both of his hands, the room where water has long seeped in through the ear. He places the room on top of an objective lens. An eye bigger than my room looks down at me. Through the eyepiece, does the room look like the inside of a kaleidoscope? He tries rolling the room about, this way and that. Even tries blowing on it. The fragile room rocks violently every time his breath touches it. An eye bigger than a house surrounds the room. It's as though a blinking sky has descended. He turns up the magnification of the lens. Like an icy sun trying to rise, a ray of light enters this shipwreck of a room. The mass of eggs I've hidden under the wardrobe is exposed. Seaweeds are untangled. The plankton from my body that fills the teardrop to the brim is found. Like a diver he combs through the inner contents of the teardrop. Inside my head, a vortex rises as though a cork has been popped off. The one I summoned, waking in the middle of the night, swirls me around at will. Unable to hold up any longer, the room of water bursts. A teardrop flows down my face and spreads. The sea wave that shakes my shoulders eats almost all of this dark room away. Outside the window where day breaks from afar, a man small as a dot passes by, a dog in tow.

Now even my chest is parched like a mummy. I lack even the strength to drink sorrow. The mere scent of water makes me shudder.

Cars trail long red tails behind them as they speed through pools of water, but why am I now climbing the Andes alone under the blazing sun? Why are birds flying up from a bonnet of fire in the western sky? Why did the mummy in the Lima Museum have a damp face even in death?

Though night has come, my car's windshield wipers continue valiantly to hang cold wet towels on their foreheads. Why am I still climbing the Andes mountains, so high that not even a blade of grass will grow? Though I climb over one after another, why do the mountains never end? Why is the mummy still hugging her parched chest with both arms? Why are her ten fingers still wet, like a lump of clay left untouched for a moment in the midst of shaping?

When flowers of rain rush into bloom like crowns of water before falling, only to be raised hastily again over the car's hood, why is the car standing still, like a cup placed upside down? Why did it stop blankly while turning a street corner? Why has the mummy come to a standstill? Why does she stand with her head cocked to the side while climbing the Andes where the raging blizzard doesn't end?

Why have I lived so long in one body puffing air like a lungfish? Am I sighing under this heavy dress? Are my eyes open? Are they closed? This evening of pelting rain, why do the vast Andes stretch before me again and again?

A Bloody Clock

There's a clock in my chest that ticks a lifetime
without stopping even once.
A clock that eats blood and shits blood,
whose red veins branch out
all over my body
like the naked vines of ivy in winter
surrounding the cement clock on the steeple.

I've never been able to make your clock ring.
No one has ever touched
my bloody lump of a clock.
Does a clock have thoughts, even brutal ones?
Who was it that taught me
a century is short and a day is long?

Once I fainted glaring at the sun's clock.
Once I hurled into the sea
my body that enfolded a clock
but no shock
no love
could ever stop this clock.
Our family of three, all showing different times
because of our different starting points,
sit around a table, silently feeding the clock
none among us has unfastened
and laid on the table,
not yet.

Ah ah, I put my lips to your ears with all my strength
to shout I love you
so that even your clock may hear,
so that your clock might ring.
But the words I love you,
the ticking of three o'clock in the afternoon

that says you love me, is it true?
We've never entered our own clocks.
When the wind howls violently outside my clock,
red vines of winter ivy
tremble in the wind inside my body
and tears gather in my eyes.
Even if only for a moment, can you stop
the hands of my clock for a short while?
Can you embrace this clock without hands?

When I put my ear to your chest,
I hear the sound of a bloody clock caught up in its heavy rhythm.
It rings on time

YR

No Hyegyông
(b. 1958)

Why I Write

When I was young, I wished for the ability to keep silent.

Fascinated by all that I saw and unable to close my mouth, I realized when night came that I'd gabbed enough to empty myself; my dreams filled my emptiness with the complicated colors of penitence. Like a girl dancing in red shoes, an unstoppable torrent of words. The priest told me it was a type of grace, but afraid that insects rather than pearls would suddenly come out of my mouth, I spent more and more nights secretly trembling. Fake flowers. Insects.

Words became difficult one day, because of a stone.

It was during the time when I walked daily across pebbled streets from the school gate to the porch of my house. I had the sudden sensation that the bottoms of my feet were vanishing and something like warm air, something unseen, shot forth.

When I looked down, a pebble was talking to me.

It winked with a certain frequency inside my head.

I couldn't translate what it said.

Chattering had been my greatest joy; spending days in silence became my greatest grief. I began to hold inside things that could not be spoken. Silence of stone. Until I could speak on behalf of stone, I'd be stiff like stone, and an emptiness old as stone sat inside me.

Is there a word heavier than silence? Can it be found?

Now, after a long time, I chatter again.

Now I worry that fake flowers will bloom from my lips. I stand with my lips against the real world created by the Lord. My wish for tomorrow morning is no longer silence. Stone slowly cools inside me. Turning into a pebble, it finally becomes weight, makes me thin, takes blood from my fingers. As old as earth, the pebble will regret how it left its body to meet me.

And then one day, suddenly waking from sleep, crying oh no oh no, unable to give voice to my longing, I cry. . . .

I'll speak of a bird remembering how it was once a bird.

It was a bird once, a bird whose wings, without strong winds, became heavier the higher it tried to rise. It was on a list of "common birds from eagles to swallows."

As for me, I'm a myna bird. Without ever spreading my wings, I strayed briefly from the right path and lost my bird nature. My genetic makeup irrevocably changed.

Entering the bird's memory, I wanted to lift toward that moment when it took to the wind and soared fearlessly, following the path of a delicate wind that I couldn't see, rising higher and higher.

No, I can't! I can't follow you. My feeble wings protested. My heart exploded.

Quietly crouched in a corner of the earth, the bird remembers its single flight. I can't see the crack between the two worlds that broke its wings. Though its fallen shape is more like a lump of crumpled writing paper than a bird, now and then, when it gets dark, its wings shine. *Sarûrûrû.*

I sob and shout that I'm satisfied with my life.

Song of Mary

They say she was sixteen when the angel of annunciation came to her. People seem to have become adults quickly back then. But it's extreme to think she could give an answer that would turn her life upside down. It would be more correct to say that she was too young to realize the weight of her decision. If that relieves your mind, call it that. Then forget it.

But nowhere in the scriptures does it say that her answer was hasty. She believed only that the strength of an unknown that lets a virgin conceive was governing her time, her history.

That means Christ's great work was already half complete in his mother's womb. Then or now, the God of the believers is powerless before those who do not believe. But the son fed on his mother's faith could not see God's empty place in his sky. He could have thought that misarranged faith, miscolored faith, filled his sky and that even when these bad faiths nailed him, it was only a matter of time. That after a long time everyone would know.

After that passed 2,000 years.

A physician irritated at having to pay her medical association and alumnae dues makes the annunciation. Then continuously asks, "Are you keeping it?"

The twenty-nine-year-old woman cannot answer confidently. "I'll consult my husband," she says, halfway up. As she exits the hospital, a smile rises on her lips. This Mary who has only the smile in common with the woman of 2,000 years ago calculates quickly in her head. That's right, his monthly salary should be raised. He'll also be promoted. If we withdraw our installment deposit, we could get a bigger place. It's about time for a child.

If only her husband doesn't lose his job, if only her husband's brother succeeds in his business, if only her sister-in-law sends money home from America to support her father-in-law.

Placing all the if onlys on the counter, she stares blankly into the sky. That place where countless neon crosses shine brightly. The only angel who would speak to her is mute.

Triangle, Mirror

We two women's eyes meet
and share our hearts' secrets.
The earrings received from the same man,
the similar lips and smiles

One woman always inside the mirror
the joy of stealing glances
the woman flattened by the mirror, flattened
like a sticker of the world outside the mirror

That man gradually flows toward the right
that woman gradually flows toward the left
suddenly that man meets my eyes
the woman at the summit of a place unseen,
the vigilant gaze glaring

Life inside the mirror is peace
life without pestering bodies
But must I go outside the mirror?
That woman
and I
must we exchange our lives?

Triangle, Comb

Realization came from a small thing

On my head
a hand
through hair
fingers enter
thick fingers enter like a comb

Pressing upon the wet eyelashes
I held my breath

Was it okay to be so friendly
quicker than reflection
I cut the hair
should I have cut the neck, too?

Combing the short hair
the tough, dull matching hand
though the hand wanted to touch
fine long hair, already gone

Perhaps
what needed to be cut was the hand
letting down the long hair

I could have washed my own feet
should I have let it grow long?

So many blades land on my hair

Memory of Underdevelopment

A strange wind blows from somewhere
a womb full of baby insects from an unknown star
with each step pain rises
out of quiet night

Emptiness filled with the pulse of a code
my antennaeless ears in discomfort
only roam the autumn road

My bones rattle inside my sacklike body.
Still in search of a nail to hang on, my soul flutters like a dirty cloth

So that's it
It's the night before birth

The antennae of insects searching for daily bread
drill through the womb and raid my skeleton

That's really it.
Some kind of monster will be born tonight.

Miscellaneous Bouquet

Meditate on jagged things
melancholy evening watching the sunset, suddenly a laugh
the moment when a long laugh runs dry and turns to silence
beside the yellow flower beside the red flower, beside the purple,
the white, the big flower, beside the nail of my pinky
bouquet like a disheveled madwoman
half dried up, half withered
bouquet filling up the trashcan
like a worn bag carried anywhere

You,
you know?

About discolored things

About the friend you wish was not your friend
about the ugly fingernail
especially about the ugly fingernail

Unable to speak to anyone
in the end sitting on my windowsill, covered with dust
you grew more lovely as you withered
and now come in as fragrance and sit

Disease That Arrives at Death

Abraham's God appeared to me
Magdalene, offer me your Isaac,
he said

Bearing anxiety and happiness
I climbed the mountain

(Please say one word, and my soul will be healed)

Silence all around
wind didn't blow, his word collected
I waited and waited
for the lamb's cry beneath the thicket to be heard
night fell
when stars shook with fright and sand muttered the sound of silence
my knife, bearing the decision, silently
but deeply
pierced
Isaac's throat

Blood fell and from drop by drop
countless lambs were born
my Isaac where are you
I was crying out and he asked
who was your Isaac?

A loose-haired woman driving the herd of sheep toward me
received my lamb into her bosom
child, newborn child
here is your mother

Happy Walk

Deep night. On a small road through the woods
I walked.
From my bones
pieces of flesh fell
like leaves. I heard the sound.

Who knows what remains
though the heart still beating is heard.
I walked endlessly here
far, I came too far.

Flapping tattered flesh, hanging
like an old wooden clapper
clattering inside a temple bell

It doesn't matter that nothing remains
but the memory of walking endlessly
inside memory, countless footprints and shadows

The brilliant shine of dark bones
the night road
lit by old phosphorescence

It was like that
perhaps it was a walk in my former life

Where the road seems to end
I telephone myself
to say it looks like the road has ended
and I don't flap
but in spattering drops
collapse

Face

Suddenly below my ankles
A dark river flows
I look down quietly
at lapping water in flames

(Die, die without a sound)

Inside the body first the bones
as if saying they know it all
little by little
settle down

That's right, this must be it
like a temple prostitute
waiting for a husband who will hold my wrist
nervously prepare oil for the lamp

But in the end fingers fall off one by one
and the prettiest
the only pretty
toenail falls off

Oh, in the end even the heart empties.
Up to the earlobes
a tear from an absent mouth stretches,
a woman with a blank face laughs

How beautiful, you
your blank face
beneath the dark river
you things that rise in flames

Wedding

Inside the womb-like darkness
the bride cries behind her veil
the procession that will have to pass by her womb
fights for the front seat and tears fall among the throng
bitter tears awake the sleeping babies
and they grow scales before they are even born
the smell of green fish
my womb's door is too narrow
I cry for the babies I will have to lose
the wedding veil is dyed in darkness
supplejack fruit's bitterness
rises on the sunset and spreads
even if the groom doesn't arrive
the womb opens
busy-hearted humanity streaming along

Children on Top of the Hill

When I enter, the hotel looks like a huge mushroom on a hilltop, divided
into thirds; shaped like a grand behind, the third-floor lobby
supports the guest floor, the hallway bends to the left, doors open in
succession, in each room couples busy making babies pause to let me
pass, I have to go to the top, I need to give a blessing,
being both busy and at rest.
Fourth floor, then suddenly eighth.
In the left corner of a room shaped like a long corridor, there's a
woman bleeding. The river of blood below wets my ankles, takes
someone somewhere; all men sit, backs turned, inside a room
warm as a tomb,
stroking the backs of men.

Sister I came, I go here

This hotel is too old
for me: sister, sibling, older sister
walking the beaches for thousands of years I must have been like a heap
of bones covered with dust by the time I reached the hotel.

(Do you know the name of this bone? a worn-out
woman asks as she strokes her shin.)

I'm going to go down again. If I spiral down the barely visible steps
the stone palace hotel will turn into a squeaky treehouse and seeds of
children collecting at the bottom for thousands of years will sprout
inside the dust of thousands of years.
When I place my hand on a rotten plank a door appears. The door must
definitely be taken off.

Pus of clay pours out.
Grotesque and lovely children of clay
are dragged out, each holding a clay doll like themselves.
Struggling against birth and still clay breaks into water.

That's right, I came to this point.
Spreading out the skirt, trying to embrace this many children between the legs, hotel of thousands of years.

Fish and Sauce

To shell and eat you, I brought all kinds of condiments. Grill, to
        grill and eat you.
Not knowing that you mere fish would stare straight at me.

Pushing aside the scales
shaking its tail
oily fragrance of fish nears

Me? You're
 going to eat me? Opening its large mouth

My long hours called life become sparkling
sauce. Become delicious sauce.

On the shelf attached to the window breakfast is spread
ohhh, a pair of silver plates

On top
well-grilled fish
without entrails, without scales

What in the world, the fish is smiling

Fish, delicious mother
delectable son

AC

Hwang Insuk
(b. 1958)

Why I Write

My mind is too lazy. Just like my body.

There's no philosophy in my poetry. Just as in my life.

In my life and in my poetry, there's no "Why." Therefore, also no "Because. . . ."

At most a "how" that's a languid, faint "sense of existence like that a cat may possess."

At most . . .

Yes, there are many realistic/unrealistic reasons that I write poetry. But I've thought of one reason why it's all right for me to write poetry!

I hope it's not in the same vein as the ridiculous sophism that insists that inexperience is my experience and that antiphilosophy is my philosophy. It's that I can't say a "sense of existence like that a cat may possess" is "At most. . . ."

Dance of Death

It's a long autumn day
when sunlight dozes, yellow,
by the graves on the breast of a hill.
Bulrushes blow as if waving,
reeds and purple eulalia, too.
Full in the sky and on the spur of the hill,
blue and yellow feathers scatter about.
The occupants of the graves wake up
and slightly, slightly open their eyes.
Ah, it's such
an autumn day.
A certain bird flies away
crying *tchorong tchorong.*

Beneath Her Ribs

I'm told beneath her ribs
is a haunted house.

I know a red centipede
lives there.

That rascal somehow settled in
without causing any harm.
The woman can't reach it—
so, one way or another,
they manage to get along.

I know a red centipede
lives there.

But as though sending a telegram
to inform her that he's well,
sometimes, without warning, that rascal bites.
Have you seen how she suddenly shudders
from the sting to her heart?

I know a red centipede
lives there.

Luckily the rascal is a sleepyhead,
but when the wind blows
he opens his red eyes and,
disturbed, raises his head.

Oh pray,
that when the wind blows
that woman's hand
gropes for a pack of cigarettes.

I know a red centipede
lives there.

All Dreams Are Sexual

I trudged along a road
where weeds randomly grew.
In the sky, a cow-shaped cloud slowly moved.
I felt thirsty.
The thick root of an old tree was lying in the bushes,
like a jar with jagged edges.
Something seemed to move, so I drew near.
A branch sprouted from that root.
A brown deer lifted its head,
its one eye made of a tree knot.
A deer, half tree, rose from a tight hole.
When its chest appeared, I realized it was an owl.
The owl, fluttering, flew up.
Watching it fly away,
I realized it was a deer.
The deer with the tree knot eye glanced at me,
flew, as if limping, then jumped away.
The four corners were penetrated by piercing silence.
At a coffee shop
resounding with a hot dance tune
near Tansông Theater,
Dr. Freud, who'd heard my story,
confidently interpreted my dream:
"All dreams are sexual."

When He Said "Soul"

He said "soul."
Like first snow falling in autumn sun,
like a foreign language,
like the mother tongue heard in a foreign land,
that word, soft and fresh,
sinks into my ear.

A yellow taxi just passing by
is still and transparent.
Sunlight enfolds
air that enters with a click.
Sunlight slops into my bosom,
and in the twinkling of an eye
raises my soul
and engulfs it in fresh air.

A coffee cup, white table, window,
and street outside sway, as if in water.
When, by chance, in conversation,
he uttered the word "soul,"
fallen leaves repeated, "Soul," "Soul."

He said "soul,"
a word that's,
yes, very strong.
Sunlight fragrant as orange!
Wind adds acidity to blood
My blood cells, part sunlight,
spin like a billion pinwheels.

A New Year's Card

I can't understand myself,
not my mind but my actions.
Unable to control them, like someone with palsy in the hand,
I crumple in front of you.
That voucher indicates the end of a portion of my life.

That portion doesn't leave all at once;
a person, a person, a thing, a thing,
some leave early,
some late,

Countless curtains in our lives,
a curtain for each thing,
curtains for my face.

Oh I wish I could always be beautiful
to each person and thing I meet.

I mumble to myself
as if to a priest or a taxi driver
and to you,

Happy New Year!

I'm Surplus

It seems my life now is surplus.
It seems that way.
I'm like a greenish shoot
on a dead branch,
placed there by mistake.
I keep waiting.
If someone snapped it off,
that person would see a sapless stem,
and, surprised, throw it away.
Now I'm
like a dead branch,
blood cells swept by the wind like leaves.
Ah, I'd like to
tug at
expectation.

Sorrow Wakes Me

Sorrow wakes me.
Already!
Sorrow that comes to wake me every dawn
comes earlier and earlier.
Clearly sorrow works too hard—
it shakes me quietly, watches over me while I wake,
bows to me reverently, and stays with me all day.
Sorrow leaves me lying for a short while,
sings to me of what happened yesterday, the day before
        yesterday, the day before the day before yesterday,
sorrow's low, husky voice makes me burst into tears,
sorrow sighs lightly and stops its song,
and asks me what I plan to do today.
I don't know, I mumble.

Sorrow raises me up,
opens the window, and folds the blanket.
Sorrow opens a book for me, receives a phone call,
warms water for washing up,
and carefully asks if I want breakfast.
I don't want to eat food prepared by sorrow.
Sorrow follows me in my outings,
but disappears every now and then.
Walking toward my room, step by step,
I know sorrow waits patiently,
crouched, filling the room.

Two Doors

Dad, how good it would have been
if that house had two doors.
Your door made a very stubborn sound,
opening and closing.
What tactlessly rustled
were only trees, it seemed.
Lying in my room
I imagined many doors.
I dreamed of a door
your ears couldn't reach.
If you faintly knit your brow,
instead of standing up to you,
my whole heart used to bleed.

Nights, roads rest,
warm winds burn.
I loved going out at night
even without a man.
Dad didn't sleep
but waited for me.
Dad, was it because
of your love for me?

Dad, if I'd had my own door
a secret door
without sound or trace,
how good would it have been?
How sweet might we have been
to each other?

I wanted to run away
jump stealthily over the wall.
Night spreads endlessly.
Dad no longer waits for me;
he sleeps.

Huge Mouth

I see pictures of the dead
in a magazine, a new book,
and on the newspaper wall.
I see, unfamiliarly, the familiar faces.
Suddenly, their words float up in print—
commas, quotation marks, periods, question marks . . . words gone by.

Voice, voice, the words' green water
doesn't return.
From faraway clouds, particles of voices
don't fall as rain.

I place my palm to my mouth
and shout ah! ah!
In the brisk wind,
warm breath, my voice
are blown far away.

Suddenly like a bone, I'm thrown
into a wind untouched by living beings.

Departed souls of voices I miss, yet unfamiliar,
the hall where their ashes were laid to rest,
that far-off sea.

A Walk

I slap on the buttonwood tree with the palm of my hand
My palm resounds
th'ông th'ông th'ông
th'ông th'ông th'ông th'ông th'ông
th'ông th'ông th'ông
Dark cockscombs, yellow marigolds, beside the ragged flower bed
I walk *th'ông th'ông*

Who rustles there?

Wind touches my body,
my blood is swept like sand,
I'm quietly being swept.

Who rustles there?

The buttonwood tree is cold, soft, and thin
I slap on the buttonwood tree with my palm
th'ông th'ông th'ông
I knock on streetlight, waste bin, motorcycle.
Beneath my feet the pavement booms,
the moon, too, booms in the sky

Who rustles there?

PL

Chŏng Hwajin
(b. 1959)

Why I Write

The countless photo negatives that don't get printed, even as generations pass. The landscapes of dreams that send us messages from bundles of images we cannot see beyond because they form our collective unconscious. The riverbank landscape that resembles the texture of the soul, and a sandy field, and also the structure of streams. A desolate beach over yonder.

Dry swamps of wet land embracing every river's course. The outer world of some star where there are dust storms. A clean yard. Water plants that rise to the surface of murmuring waves in the heart. A sea that embraces flames and tidal waves and harbors storms. . . .

Phrases that go, "Everything is a neon light in the world below ice." Sad souls who don't hesitate to be reborn. The wind that stirs small leaves. A crimson peony blooming in a garden.

Ah. . . .

I wouldn't have been able to express the nature of the real heartbreak that's afflicted the short life dealt to me without the medium of poetry. In this world of wealth and weariness, only in the province of poetry could one long-abandoned existence dispatch mutual understanding— or misunderstanding—while sending a message of distress in a low, stammering voice, to the far interior of the world.

Dance

Billions of maggots are being sucked into a whirlpool.

Al hal ral ral rai

Ral ral ral hai hai

Al hal ral ral rai

A Knife Gets Bigger

3:10 A.M. I get up and go to the kitchen. I see it while looking for a glass of water.

It's still. Sounds as slight as pomegranate seeds are rooted in the darkness.

I'm thirsty. A new moon seeps through the kitchen window. A blue-green light flickers on an overturned cup.

For a moment, the knife barely gleams.

Past the cup, in the corner overlooking the sink, the knife lies placidly on the cutting board.

The knife gets bigger. . . . July heat. The ground is yellow, and the shadow of the mulberry bush by the low part of the earthen wall appears short.

A young girl rests near the sill, her thin neck leaning straight against it.

The knife draws near. The knife, with a deathly pale blade, in Grandmother's hand scrapes against the doorway.

Grandmother washes the knife in clean water from the gourd dipper she has filled.

The girl, who'd been drinking the water the knife was washed in, stares at the knife, behind the counter now.

The knife gets bigger. . . .

The knife's wash water lulls heat eaten away by malaria.

The knife's small teeth are driven into the girl's chest, and she spits out malaria and the knife's wash water.

I, all grown, leave the kitchen. Thinking I've quenched my thirst, I lift the knife.

The knife gets bigger. . . . The girl is eating the knife.

The knife suddenly turns toward the cemetery and flees. Moonlight, and the chrysanthemums are blooming.

The knife gets bigger. . . .

After neatly sweeping the yard for the girl, Grandmother scratches the earth in the very middle of the yard, drawing the mark of a cross. Dusty yellow earth blows in the breeze.

Grandmother drives the knife perfectly into the center of the cross. She covers the gourd.

She'd tear the heart of malaria to pieces.

For a while, the knife flickers.

I go back to the kitchen. I pick up the knife and throw it at the window.

The knife breaks. The solid glass of the kitchen window breaks it.

I see another knife get bigger.

I feel I'm beginning to want to sharpen it.

I think I want to run to Grandmother's grave carrying the knife's wash water.

Grandmother's sunken cheek reddens, as though it would come back to life.

The knife gets bigger.

The clock tells me it's 3:15 A.M. It's still.

Slowly, the slight sounds rooted in the darkness start to fall away, one seed at a time.

The South Yard

Umm, I can't eat, Grandma. . . .
A yard where smoke rises, lifting the darkness.
A mosquito smoker still burns in the yard.

Streaming from the kitchen, the knife's gleam slashes
       the darkness-shrouded yard.
When Grandmother walks silently to the very middle of the yard carry-
       ing a wooden ladle, the countless stars that had been scattered
       all fall into the bloody water in the ladle's bowl.
The Milky Way shines askance into the south yard, and figures which
       can be seen only from behind sit around the mosquito smoker.

Over the earthen wall, there,
       mother turtles have come crawling by the base of a tree stump
       near the bank of the stream.
They cover their eggs with purple flower petals, and scatter broken
       pieces along the length of the levee in the south yard.
A still yard, where the perfume of purple flowers cloaks the turtle's
       blood in the ladle and mingles with the mosquito smoker's
       scent.
Ah. . . . How could Grandma have chopped the turtle's neck?

I shook off summer days spent shivering, and when I went to the river
       bank just before dawn, the water was overrun with the perfume of
       purple flowers surging up.

The Hidden Path

The water's surface trembles delicately,
and trees stand by the undulating shore.
Water grasses lying sidelong in the distance wilt
and rise in the breeze.
By the shore, shattering sunbeams.

A water strider draws a circle on the water and takes cover in a forest of
water grass.

The shivering water's surface now lies open, calm.
For a moment, water grasses along the edges stir.
Below them,
the fine sand plain grows suddenly cloudy.

Leaving a slanted water trail behind, a goby minnow hides its tail in the
water grass and disappears. The cloudy water clears and its surface
shakes.

In the water,
several narrow paths
wind above the soft sand field.
It is still. Clear, open.

A Bowl of Mul Kimch'i[1]

A bowl of *mul kimch'i*
set on the dinner table with a splash.
Eating a spoonful of floating pickled cabbage,
I suddenly see pale green
issue forth from inside the bowl,
and a persimmon tree in Usan-ni springs up.

Inside the bowl of *mul kimch'i,*
between the pickled leaves,
two mountain birds alight on an upper branch
of the deep-set persimmon tree
and the knobby mountain ridge swells
toward the persimmon tree's top.

Broken twigs soak the rice spoon I dropped into the bowl
while stirring the branches of the persimmon tree.
The mountain birds, fluttering, fly off,
and in the distance, only the sky of Usan-ni[2] streams down
atop the dinner table where the persimmon tree has vanished.

1. *Mul kimch'i* is a water-based, spiced and fermented mixture of radish or cabbage with hot pepper powder, green onion, garlic and salt. It is one of Korea's most well-known and popular foods.
2. Usan-ni is a city in South Korea.

The Sewing Box

A kerosene lamp burns deep within an inner courtyard
where paulownia leaves rustle silently.
Through gourd flowers blooming above the stable,
a new moon descends, sweeping the dark village away.

Lamplight bathes the terrace stones and spreads into the yard.
A child sleeps peacefully below the lamplight
that grazes Grandmother's cheek.
Bits of soot swirl above the child's face,
then draw a long pattern on the ceiling before becoming faint.
Grandmother adjusts the lamp's wick
and removes a faded, yellowed collar from a full dress suit.
as a finger thimble and pieces of leftover thread are drenched
by lamplight inside the sewing box.

Disconsolate, I step into the darkened yard,
hitting a dead red-bellied frog with the tip of my toe.
The new moon, shattered, clings to the lattice, trembling faintly.
Grandmother's room, where dust and darkness intermingle now
is barely visible in the lamplight, and empty, without needle,
bobbin, or twinkling thimble. The sewing box has been set down.

Someone tears the new moon off the patterned lattice. Someone sobs.
I peer into the room. My sobbing suddenly pushes open the door.
Ah, Grandfather's suit still hangs there.
Leaving my tears in the empty room,
I stumble away from the reeling courtyard
to the crunch of paulownia leaves, the sewing box in my hands.

I'm a Dragonfly Caught in a Net

Grandfather disappears into a field. The yard is empty. Silent threads of sunlight stream down. Grazing a bush clover hedge, a dragonfly, quivering, alights, a dragonfly. A dragonfly, a child catches the dragonfly with a dragonfly net. I'm a dragonfly. My whole body shudders. Caught in a net, I await the cat. A mottled cat approaches. Inside the net, I'm yellow. The cat's eyes are yellow. The cat's teeth devour the dragonfly's eyes. I go into the cat with a rasping sound. The moon rises. Caught inside the child's net, the dragonfly's wings, wings are caught. I wait for Grandfather. The moon rises on the field.

Sunlight Showers Down in Sheets

It falls into the water with a gurgle. Bubbles rise to the top and burst.
      Eyes open in the bright light.
The back legs of a water beetle gently clear a path. Sunlight showers
      down in sheets on the water.
Sands roll, tumbling over the edge. A shining white belly,
      discernible through the water grass, sunlight fastened
onto fish scales, a fragile fin flutters. Sunlight passes through
      a freshwater shrimp's transparent flesh.
The sands turn over lightly.
Sunlight showers down on a floating school of black-eyed fish.

Suddenly, the Yard Where Rice and Yeast Brew

The child clings to the prettily patterned lattice.
The child's eyeball falls out and disappears. Shutters close.
Moving over the floor, the sound of a sliding door clears noises spread over the yard. Sound trembles. The door shakes. Shutters open. Inside the half-open door, you can see the child. The child's face is red.

A violet-colored jar sits there. Something is brewing inside. On the jar's upper part, roundly wrapped in a pattern of stripes so tenuously aligned they might break apart, the small handprints of a child are smeared. Foam bubbles over the edge. The room where rice and yeast brew. Noises that burst drop by drop pass through the door and fall into the yard. Red-tinged purslane in the garden's corner explodes with flower seeds. Flying off to the peach orchard, the twinkling seeds pass branches and land on the ground, listen to the sounds streaming from the yard. The child is sleeping, drunk on wine. In the kitchen, Grandmother gathers hot coals. The room is hot. The scent of yeast permeates the yard. Sunlight crookedly penetrates the peach trees' branches. The upper branches shake.

Outside the earthen wall that suddenly brightens, peach trees burst into bloom. Drunken serpents spew rainbows forth.

Monsoon Season Opens Children's Eyes

Rain fell without stopping.
Each crock filled to the brim, and,
well, children were immersed in the water.
Isn't this a strange dream, miss?

The children at the window opened their eyes,
and three bitterlings swam past the gardenia tree, waving their tails
and pulling the stream along behind.
The fine edges of their back fins trembled.
Swaying, children's eyelashes drifted onto the water. Breaking the crock,
the children swam out to the stream. Bitterlings infiltrated the crock.
Overnight, bubbles filled it.
The perfume of gardenia brimmed out.

But that's not the truth.

It was a fish egg, sister-in-law!

It only creeps into the dreams of children who want to go to the river.
Monsoon season lays eggs in our dreams,
makes children open their eyes,
wear fragrant wings,
and cry bitterly inside the water,
and makes us, each day, lay empty crocks around the yard.

Water in a Gourd

The round gourd dipper could scoop up my cheek.
But I was still a bride.
Dawn peered in prettily.
Trembling, my whole body shivered.

The sky slanted and opened several times.

JP

Yi Yônju
(1953-1992)

Born in 1953 in Kunsan, North Chôlla, Yi Yônju made her debut as a poet in the fall of 1991 at the age of thirty-eight. A year after the publication of her first collection, *Night Market with Prostitutes* (1991), Yi committed suicide. Her posthumous work, *Atoning Sheep, Judas*, was published shortly thereafter.

Yi saw the dark shadows of industrial society and gilded civilization, the alienated and repressed, and the breakdown of family, shame, and pretense. Chosen to attract attention, her images include decomposing corpses, putrid smells, rotting blood, and pus—all associated with corruption, sickness, and death. In her work she likens herself to a salted mackerel and a sewer. The passage from birth to death, she says, is as easy as throwing a fistful of hair into a garbage can, and it is better to die in the womb than to be born. Struggling to withstand the madness of society that threatens to engulf her, she asks radical questions about all the established modes of life. Ultimately death seemed the only escape from the absurdity she saw around her. Following the wish expressed in her suicide note, her ashes were scattered in the North Han River.

A Clinic in a Dangerous Season I

—Anonymous Love

I'd really love to become a flower, or clouds—
a flower that says, "Perhaps I love you nine times more than you love me."
clouds that, donned in feathery garb, outrun you on your way back home.

The evening newspaper, though delivered, has no meaning.
Neither dead cats nor ghosts of rats
linger around the gate anymore—
the love of a flower or of clouds.

The government would surely keep it secret—
mob psychology, once contaminated by love,
would make their strategies troublesome.
But the air feels it, and surely the wind feels it, too.

If I scatter flower pollen into the sky
calling you out, my love,
the air will brighten.
How happy that feathery garb will make the sky,
because, you know, it's love.

A Clinic in a Dangerous Season 7

—The Moving of a Warm Space

I'm alone here, but
someone may be fast asleep, sunk in sweet, deep sleep,
even sleep-talking in his dream.
Or could it be showers of large-flaked snow?

In the snowfall, the winter night summons the window's
         memories of rain
and intones a requiem.
Startled, I ask, "Is that you?"

I'm alone, indeed,
there's no one else but—

Is that you, your warm sleepy breath cuddling cold air,
even while you talk in your dream?

A Clinic in a Dangerous Season 8
                    —A Scapegoat, Judas, and an Extraterrestrial

In a corner of the barn where juice oozes out of rotten fruit
and swarms of maggots and rice weevils crawl,
I met you, a resident of Venus, who, out of the blue,
dropped down alone without even riding a UFO.

When my father is lost in television in the main room,
and my mother, beside him, has fallen into a doze
yearning for my sister, divorced and in a far off land,

I drink the sour milk of time,
and you, a Venusian, run a fever for me,
your body erupting with spots.

As in the Last Supper, I love you;
so, like Judas who sold Jesus and died of a ruptured gut,
what if I pray deep in the piles of jagged rocks
among alien crowds

with my tender heart throwing up blood?
You, a being from Venus,
with simple eyelids,
you'd love me
with an albatross love, the kind found in your land far beyond the west.

I wonder why you're here beside me,
on this meteor called Earth,
even as you lick the neck and thigh
of this amputated land—
flesh sunk in despair, resentment, and gloom.

Judas does not complete himself.

Our Old Home

Lungs have countless globules, you know, like bunches of
        grapes.
Irritation or bad weather may trigger them to cough.

Beauty, how simple it can be—
the breath of the mist swimming around sockets of bone,
the energetic pulse of vessels filled with blood.
There, even salty winds—
or those fitful naps in back rooms sustained by twisted love—
once they reach there, will replace dim bulbs.
Many a time the path of our life meanders,
but imagine, our old home has been there all along in us!

But why then
do I cough so much?
Maybe paper flower petals fill my lungs.

An Open-Eyed Blind Man

At the mere sound of rushing wind,
a cataract-stricken blind man, open-eyed,
is startled and trembles violently.
His withered body hides inside a worn-out coat,
and with dull, gray, open eyes,
he gropes for a stick and goes to the corner of the room,
where he shudders, then shudders again.
How many years has his small window rattled in the north wind?
Days and nights, quilt pulled over his head,
he doesn't even want to know whether today
the sun set after drying wetlands somewhere,
whether someone was tried and sentenced,
whether someone died, nameless, again,
or whether someone somewhere poured gasoline over his body
         and raised a flag;
his whitish window merely blinks as if in convulsion.
The ugly, open-eyed, cataract-ridden blind man, who even in his dreams
pulls the hardened loaf of bread toward his pillow—
no one pays any attention to him now—
the one, who, one day,
having hidden his body in the loose and worn-out coat,
scratched out the black pupils of his own eyes,
to turn a blind eye to the world.

For the Sake of Two Screws

A man got stuck in the door;
he can't take a single step.
Beside him, a man with fierce, slanted, eyes is also trapped.
Of course, he, too, can't budge an inch, either inside or out.
They're like filled lamps
swinging amidst confusion and wandering.

The one leaning against the door speaks,
and his words resemble aphasia.
He seems to be lost, although he goes on and on.

The other man deciphers the codelike utterances.
It's difficult.
In the end, there's no way but to read them as he likes.

He reads, but I'm at a much deeper place.
He reads, and I want to be swung
just one more time.
One of them smiles at the other ghost-like man.

There are two men.
Both are stuck in the door.
They ought to get out one way or another,
break either the door or themselves.

Like clouds of old days,
like winds of old days,
like skies and earth of old days.

The man closes his fierce, slanted eyes—
if they were fired up by anger,
they need to remain closed for a long time.

Grandmother's Sea

Grandmother walked over
and became coral.
Lying in an unmarked grave,
after forty years alone,
she gazed up at the sunken moon,
and her eyes got red.

Each day she hangs an arching rainbow
over mountains and across the sea's horizon,
and waits for a boat to weigh anchor, sail away.
All her life, she dedicates her eyes
on an altar of waves.

My two ears prick up
at the soft sound of footsteps, of rubber shoes,
taking with them the sound of the sea.

Taking a Watermelon as a Paradigm

The questions:
whether to live
or die, to fight
or give up—

Facing a large watermelon,
afraid to cut it,
I turned it round and round
until those questions reached my mind.

Great are they who, for hopeless causes,
wage a battle and give up their lives—
the greatness of youthful warriors!

At the touch of the blade,
the watermelon cracks open
and reveals its ripe, red flesh.
My whole being
thrown at your
green body.

Holiday Inside an Incubator

I.
A relapse of my stomach problem—
a foreboding gloom.
"I'd like to be healthy," says the suicide
from the picture hanging on the wall.
"I'd like to be your friend."

2.
Two o'clock—
time locked between the window and its frame—
I hang on the laundry line
like fish bones.
. . .
What would it mean to have no fear of death?

3.
The headline in today's evening paper reads
WHO MISTREATED HIM AND SENTENCED HIM TO LIFE IN PRISON?
I kill a poisonous moth.
Why do I find beauty only in negation?
Pieces of soap hardening in Auschwitz.

The Bread and I

As you bake in the oven, wafting sweet scent,
I peer into the bathroom mirror
and cut off a fistful of hair.
In the mirror, a pistol moved like the cursor on the computer monitor,
dragged up forever into sky.

Rising from the breakfast table until time for the next meal,
these hands, which have hidden secretly rotting flesh,
wander from one train station to another to scalp tickets—
my endless dedication to stories of desire and wandering—
damn it!

Now, the bread is baked.
On one piece, a lump of jam,
on another, a piece of smoked human flesh—
but the tearless meal has no harmony, no joy.

Oh, bread,
I'm a fool, shoveling empty sky.
Isn't it better to turn around?
It's time for the bullet's embrace.

The glass window shatters to pieces by itself,
and the gravity inside the mirror breaks.
Oh, to be worthy of a lefty's name,
where should I aim my firery round?

YK

Yi Sanghûi

(b. 1960)

Why I Write

For me, it's either too cold or too hot outside, too crowded or too barren, too tall or too low, too mechanical or too emotional, too complex or too simple. When I must go out, I'm frightened. So I either prepare myself fully or set out waving a white flag.

Poetry, for me, is a safe way of withstanding the outside world and also a way in which I expose myself to it, accept the outer space. The song of a person trapped in a prison a thousand kilometers deep, enrapturing, like instinct, and sung with the whole body.

My poem is my screaming voice.

Dracula

Please draw the fear bigger
Deep inside my eyes
Fangs flash
I must go now
I'm anemic
I'm very dizzy
When the wind blows like this
I can't endure it
Someone's blood is
Calling me
In no time, my teeth
Are stuck in a beautiful woman's neck
Hot discharge of mixed blood
My lips are enflamed
Like ashes,
Blow cooled-off smoke
At that moment
I have to pretend I know fear

Van Gogh

It was a blue night;
I smeared hot mud
on my forehead.
The crazy moon rose
and I began to use sign language.
It was in the wind
rolling up trees *woo woo*
like blazing flames.
Crows poured down.
The horizon crumbled.
Soul broke like a boil.
Madness like a moon
suddenly
vanished

Dickinson's Blue Sleeve

Grandmother Emily Dickinson
put me on her back, took me to the faraway ocean
to the sandy plain for the first time.
No sign of exhausted animals.
Clams were living comfortably
inside their shells.
Grandmother soaked her blue sleeve
in the ocean;
after washing my injured foot,
she put it down quietly
like silent tears.
She clapped her hands, walking backward;
I slowly walked toward her with open arms;
she laughed heartily and withdrew.
(Hold me Grandmother
like ocean waves hiding a crab.)
On the sandy plain by a faraway ocean,
no boat moored.
Grandmother Emily Dickinson
Her maiden laughter
alive, intact.

As My Will Concurred Not To My Being,
It Were But Right and Equal to Reduce Me to My Dust[1]

Desire consumes hunger; hunger consumes blind jealousy
Blind love consumes a finger that pledged an oath; a ring
      consumes a maiden
and is satiated, unable to go back,
unable to escape that dark ring

Bitten in the tail, dragging the nightmare around
What are you living on?

1. John Milton, *Paradise Lost*, Book 10.

Dance

When I wait
for more tears to well up,
from a body that like a dried flower,
has no tears,
I dance.
In the empty space of night
between chimes of the clock,
my heart collapses with a thud.
Rusted joints
applaud.
Soon tears well up.

Again I twist my waist
until I fall into a dreamless sleep
Like a sadness that neither sinks nor soars
I dance
like a body that forever has no tears,
like a picked flower that, for three days, laughs.

Organizing a Drawer

Blue eraser dust
Collected
Inside the dark straws of memory
Inside my almost-lover's business card
Inside exposed film
Inside an unused theater ticket
Inside a letter never sent
Inside overdue tax notices

When will I dust them off?

For Men to Tell How Human Life Began Is Hard, For Who Himself Beginning Knew?
Desire With Thee Still Longer to Converse Induced Me as New-Waked from Soundest Sleep
Soft on the Flow'ry Herb I Found Me Laid in Balmy Sweat[1]

Tears, in the end,
like the waves of Malli Cove,
pushed up the eyelid of the dead heart,
enabling me to run again
on love's rough, sandy plain.

1. John Milton, *Paradise Lost*, Book 8.

A Morning Stroll

A cold
Dead face is
Inside my pocket
Memories
Strewing
Dried breadcrumbs
Lost the way
But
The clump of hair
Inside the pocket
Is still warm,
Thawing my frozen hands

Dark windows
Layer after layer
Freezing
On an autumn day

A dead face is cold
Inside my pocket
On my way to bury
My cold face,
The dawn is
Warm

I Ask in Late Evening

Why, tonight—
the computer screen in front of me, to the left
old and faded red tile roof, to the right
layer after layer of roof—in the distance can a man be seen?
Be seen?

What's certain is
that the man in that distant space
is purgatory's clerk.

He retired early to the place between heaven and earth.
His hobby is taking care of the garden in the air
Holding the water hose, he bends down,
talking with something green

Is that flower hiding a bud?
Trees without flowers.
Am I human, or an animal who can't see clearly
from this side of the road?
Is it evening?
Is this purgatory?

I ask in late evening

Farewell, My Youth

Spit it out when sweet
Swallow when bitter
Impudent young tongue
Stretched like leather

Night, Work

Because of the tailbone
the wooden chair hurts,
simply because of that.
Everything was tiresome.
Couldn't endure.
Ah!
No scales, no water,
no flesh, feeling only the tailbone.
Breathlessly palpitating gills,
a night of gills.

Igloo! Igloo!

Igloo, igloo
My mouth is glued
Igloo, igloo
As soon as the fish jumped out of the bowl
it froze in the air
Igloo, igloo
As soon as it went down the throat
a sip of water became a long, long icicle
Igloo, igloo
A child running to be embraced
became an icicle
Igloo, igloo
Ice flower, ice chair, ice food

This ice house
It's my fault, it's my fault
My hand, about to pound my chest, froze too
Igloo!

JL

Pak Sôwôn

(b. 1960)

Why I Write

In a world without truth, where all exits are closed, the only salvation other than death is that offered to us by way of literature. For literature is the home of truth.

From childhood, I thought there was no place in the world for me to live. For me, death was the only garden that held a glimmer of hope. In adolescence, I turned my thoughts toward the question of existence, together with a newfound religious consciousness. And I loved poetry. It always had the habit of preceding me. It guided me to the place I'd been heading toward. Poetry molded me. It was poetry that had the strength to stop me from stepping backward, to start my life, and had the power to harness pain for infinite creation. Through poetry, we can represent our love of things, our imperfect existence. Writing poetry offers us a dimension of clarity, one that brings us face to face with God as an unconditional act for, and of, life.

Obsession

The knife on the fruit dish
is always ready to stab me.
The dizziness of the sick,
the softness of the sick,
never fails to seize me.

Blessed are those who wish to go mad!

A flashlight illuminates my womb.
A kiss on scarred and bloodstained flesh.
Inside, a wet face rhythmically flows.
A cormorant dives into the water.
Venomous insects that were adrift blaze up in a sea
            of candlelight.
The sea comes to rich fruition.
Red. Yellow. Emerald. Blue-green.
Colors of miracles that flash in your eyes.
The fear of miracles.
An insult, a joy.
A consummate Holy Communion.
An oar is born.
An oar.

The knife on the fruit dish
always stabs me. And always while being stabbed,
the mutilated songs. . . .

Menstrual Irregularities

I stand before the calendar and count the days.
"You can't get pregnant."
That may be true. I'm weak. I've swallowed pills for years,
but there's no doubt that I'm barren as the grassless tundra.
I want a child. I want to be a woman.
Have my menses hardened, like a life just missed?
Yes, I'll admit to that. Still, people are always ready to renew
        themselves. For now, for the sake of this new emergency,
        I'm just a resting mare. Should I say it's like the chaos before
        the creation of the earth?
Yes, my womb is a water trough that waits for rain, tomorrow's
        patient agave. A mast that rises when the tide flows and ebbs.
        An icicle that freezes and melts.
The kind that turns into ice cream.
A gentle breeze behind the dry breath
that bathes the blades of grass.
On a flaming hill,
a spotless railroad depot at the summit illuminates a new light post. . . .

Someone is whispering to me again. You can't get pregnant.
Hardly!
I whisper even more deeply into my womb. Hardly!
Now I'm looking down on the water flowing inside me,
        overflowing like a swift stream.
Children thrive and swim in the current.
I was always whole.

A Recurring Nightmare: My Amputation

A dream, a glittering saw blade. Four stumps
deep within the reed forest of convulsions inside my head.
Arms and legs that drop away.
I was as stiffly silent
as an old shoe thrown into the street.
It wasn't for the sake of silence.
It was for my quiet depravity,
heavy as an overcoat one rainy winter evening.
It was for the unnatural deaths of those four pieces
that had just been me.

My scent speaks for itself. Dreams aren't beasts.
Herald of the nether shores, the raven of death flaps its wings
        as though it were forgiving a debt I owed myself.
I stay still, lest I be caged.
Struggling would only tire me out.
Even if I could scream, only the sound would be heard.
Ahh!
The four stumps are now one.
My bloodline is hastily assembled and systematically placed,
        like a saw-toothed wheel in a huge factory.
I'm laughing.
Barbecued by my own dreams.
My scent speaks for itself. Dreams aren't beasts.

A Small Wooden Vessel

So much to load!
Swelling and surging, the sea sings its love.
I didn't even know how heavy I'd become while the cargo was
        being loaded.
I could throw it all out, one piece at a time,
Starting with the light things—one orange segment,
        a pearl.
Like sugar in the mouth, the sea melts the sun.
I've become heavy and cannot cut the anchor.
What I threw overboard still drags alongside me,
        hanging by a clear silk thread.
If only my weeping could swallow the whole sea.
The belly-boat[1] teeters, rocking and rolling the heavier it gets.
Think, I don't even have the freedom
        to throw my own possessions away.

---

1. In Korean, the words for boat and belly are homonyms, with the same spelling. Pak is drawing a homonymic connecton between the boat and the narrator's body.

The Midnight Caller

Have the waves lost their way?
This is my house in Seoul.
I open the door, my ears prick up as though I were lifting
          a kettle's lid.

"I'm a pearl,
I dislike soft, sweet things,
I'm a jewel marinated in salt.
I'm small but strong. Don't you agree?
I'm such a jewel.
The cuttlefish dried at dusk are my ladies in waiting."

Echoing with the sound of waves,
a seashell stands trembling.

I pick the seashell up in my cupped hands.
Waves crash at will.

A silk-covered lantern casts greenish light upon the street.
In the sky, the moon flutters a red handkerchief.
Desire, once so beautiful,
settles down as an elm tree.

"I'm the pearl inside the shell.
I'm standing here because I cannot speak."

To the Man Holding a Sickle

Come now, come here.
My dear mule,
I thought you were a door.

Have you heard? A revolt is breaking out.
Many can't escape the bonds of your temptation.
My tough umbilical cord, my mule, I too was enthralled by you.

Still,
come here now,
my dear baby.

For me, empty-handed, you're a great family tradition.
You sleep soundly under my blanket.
In one hand, a toy.
Can you see?
You cannot forsake me.
I tend you inside myself
on the very wheels of longing.

Come now, come here,
my beloved goldfinch.
You are limitlessly free.
      Beneath my sea,
      I take you for a walk.

The Wind God Sends Forth

The wind blows,
then rolls down the hill.
In its wake, everything that can, rolls down too.

Good-natured people
happily wave to one another,
and build new square homes.

Farmers who once plucked stones from plowed fields
are crushed beneath an avalanche of rolling things.

Blood and stones don't lie,
though falsehoods hide safely underground in a tunnel dug
       with bones.

The pens weren't always inside their case.

Whenever a festival comes to town,
forgetful brutes who shuffle and shamble about
hunt for someone to execute.
They're restless.

If the wind God sends forth is like that,
I should live on, even after death.
While I try to figure out why farmers are buried without a shroud,
the carnival comes to an end.

Smoke rises into the sky.
Again. Once more, it rolls down the hill.

In a plowed field, new farmers sit
chewing leaves,
plucking stones.

Lies

Little bitch!
I want you.
I want the broad-bosomed, big-breasted harlot
who is every husband's temple, every skeleton's whore.
So many children
born,
from a dead placenta.
May.
Covering the fence, red roses without petals.
You.
You.

Little bitch!

Look at your pretty self,
obedient as a herd of cattle.

You could lead the world.

You can understand
the loneliness of wind that blows in a deserted cemetery.
You can touch the ritual chant of departed souls.
You can really and truly love.
True love is the whore's consummate skill.

You don't know.
Your whole body is a womb
for the very teeth that gnaw at your wounds.

Ah, teeth.

Hey, little bitch!

Plantain

I saw it by chance.
Near the corner
of the house,
a plantain blossom.

The next day, we were flooded for several days
because of the monsoon.

Even after, until winter arrived,
I forgot all about it.

Then one midnight, returning home drunk,
I saw it by chance again.
Countless blooming plantain flowers.

And the first one, shriveled up dead.

The Highway

Here, it's a carless highway.
A face resembling a well-ripened persimmon zips past my head.
I'm running barefoot, trying to find a barn.
Even the horizon has disappeared.
To betray the freedom God has given me,
I tear off pieces of my flesh,
slamming into rest stops whenever I see them.
I'm speeding down the road to my sky, soft and cold as mercury.
To enjoy the freedom God has given me,
I seek a barn where an emaciated poplar tree stands,
a mad wind blows, and toxic grasses grow;
where there is a crystal-like well,
trying to accomplish a revolution.

JP

Ho Sugyông

(b. 1964)

Why I Write

Asked why I write poems, I'm filled with thoughts. And yet this isn't the question that's occupied my mind for the past decade, which I've spent studying in Germany. The question has been not why I write poems at all, but rather why I write poems in Korean, or whether I have no choice but to write in Korean. After all, the Korean language is not used outside a country called Korea, except perhaps when Korean people living abroad get together. It may be that the language in which they exhale their loneliness or suffering when they are alone is Korean rather than a foreign tonguge. For me, certainly, it's always in Korean that I talk to myself when I'm in pain. In urgent situations, Korean words invariably pop from my mouth. And when I chat with my mother on the telephone, the accents of my native Kyôngsang province never fail to creep back .

Studying the archeology of the ancient Near East, I've come across many ancient languages. The language that has particularly interested me, however, is Sumerian. Though Sumerian became a dead tongue over four thousand years ago at the end of the Neosumerian Epoch, we still remember it—and through this dead language, we're able to know the living history of an age long past. The same is true for languages other than Sumerian. Even now, in this very century, languages of myriad minority groups are becoming extinct. For why should anyone harbor any interest in languages of people without power? Why seek to learn a language, indeed to worship it, unless it can be of immediate use in one's own life?

I know that in this world of ours, my mother tongue carries no political weight. But Korean is still my tongue, the language I was raised in from birth to a being capable of expressing her thoughts. It may very well be that one day this language of mine will be forced to relinquish life as a spoken language.

And me? What about my poetry?

No one will be able to erase the fact that a certain poet lived her time and wrote poems in Korean, that she recorded her agonies and joys, her very existence in this world, in her own language. As long as I don't forsake this task, my words will live on, like the written words of countless people long disappeared.

Love in an Empty Lot

I stayed still a while.
Has love been spoiled?

Love abandons me and flows to you.
Love abandons you and flows to time.

Bright is the ancient mark of a forgotten wound,
bright and painful.

I'll go to this bright, painful place
when a painful dream fills the years again.

When the rainbow above the empty lot
fills again with pain in the flow of time,

a heart's lips without a body
will grope where a blade of grass grows
for a dream that has not attained words.

Sober, Remaining

The drinking party in spring's shade—
what year was it?
Was the sun shining then?
Did I lie in disarray in the sun?
Still, I don't recall surrendering my heart.

Did hearts look into each other?
Did I hold you,
seeking that which can be held without arms?
The borderless spring shade—
was that you?

The heart had lost its way
and wished to live in dreams and die,
drunk, alone.
But heart, why did you return,
revisiting the very road you'd traveled?
Was leaving that hard?

I didn't give my heart.
Unable to get more drunk,
I was bound
to a road on which I could neither come nor go.
I didn't want to be fine anymore
and I wasn't fine anyway.

Burying my face in spring's shade,
did I cry?
Swallowing my tears, did I start to walk again?
The only thing I don't remember is surrendering my heart.

A Weeping Singer

a singer sings and days go by
love, did you shed tears for me
still, warm were the days when I could weep
I, too, once cried out in vain—
I'm not going to die—
and spread like rays of the sun
against the stone wall of an abandoned house
though the pledge, like warmth, betrayed us
the cry of migratory birds still saddens
ooh ooh hearts touched with sorrow
ooh ooh how these hearts touch me with sorrow
worldly affairs left unexplained
so that heart straying from heart may return to heart—
they make me weep
still, the warmth of being able to weep
are you wet, too, love
the entrance I've kept hidden, the only entrance to yearning—
are you wet, too,
even the love I've lost abandons me
time, you're heartless
but I sing this paean of love

One White Dream

midday I go to the park alone
        to ask while chugging wine from a hidden bottle:
        wind, do you pity me as you drift by

        with every step, I make muscles and tendons. the footsteps I
        leave behind—a sunken interior? a gaping, open grave? ah, the
        road of drunken headache

        a broken car fills me with pity. why?
it can't move and lets nothing out
will it rot away?
        that snake breaks my heart too. why?
            its body is just a leg, even its uterus is a leg
what about its face?
           could it have been love . . . .
aha love!
that sound of the heart bolting itself, love!

        the red-beaked bird so fond of crying, where has
            it gone?
why did you go around like a blushing idiot
searching for private places to walk?
do you remember that hand?
in the end, the wine the heart has drunk makes the hand
ache
this win. . . .

a tremor moves through my tough-as-woodshavings heart. in
every storeroom: a finger, a fingerprint, a whirling eddy, solitude
in a midday park

rays of sun crush my heart in the end
you. . . .

The One At Rest

Disillusionment, did you slip from my body and return with wine?
Forsythias bloom at the tips of smarting fingers
and I...doze off, leaning against the cinderblock wall of this
world.

I...drink wine.
I used to say words like these with no one listening.
I...am drunk, shucks, like a hobo.

A single straw hut,
a single room to lay me down;
lowliness!
Little children wear sneakers that are too big for them, like lies.

Someone sings:
Burying care in every rip, wherever the sun has set
with nothing to rub against, take me with you.
Can I do that?
Take me with you.
My face makes me weep.

It must have hurt, shucks, like a hobo.
I'm fine. Above the cinderblock wall of this world
clouds scatter. The light of red lanterns hung at every house
is strewn like bits of thread,
close, like stitches from a sewing machine. Dear sister,
mother,
I'm going now, after feasting on the dazed dream of this world.

When I Think About the Past

Why does it feel like I'm dreaming
when I think about the past—
a wondrous loveliness
in the wilderness of the here and now.

Once I shuddered, thrashed, screamed,
go away, go away forever.
I didn't want to go back.
Now I long for the days when I madly raved
with all my whored affection.

And I now crawl
with all my heart and soul
toward that night of prattling wisteria blossoms,
the night of the storm.

Why does the past demand
penance for things not yet past?
Why is the only loveliness in the shade of black rock sheer cliff,
        you, only you?

Go away forever if the sky clears above Mount Inwang;[1]
go away like a dream or not even a dream.
Why does my body ache like a soul
when I remember the past?

---

1. Reference to a painting titled "Clear Sky Above Mount Inwang," by Chông Sôn
(1676–1759).

Poem

slash my back with a sickle
my back slashed, I've come this far
bring a sickle and slash my back again
my back slashed, I prepare a meal

though the sun sets raw like dripping blood
I eat
gaze at the sky
drink water
lie down

No Return

slate roof
decaying wood broken
window-glass a handful of night
breeze shoved in by the gathering
dark that reclines like a friend by beside
"No Return"

I no longer recognize
my place nor do
my close kin recognize
"No Return"

knees are damp on a morning
frosted with down
child, ain't it too far
once we there we don't wanna come back
ain't it too far
drops of sweat like red bean porridge
hemp knee breeches soiled by rays of sun
ah this head o'mine why it ache so
"No Return"

furrows in millet fields
their blind hollows suck
my slate roof in,
my wooden window frames
"No Return"

my moans
my promises
parted lips of a Chinese-pink blossom
don't return in the end
"No Return"

child, I'll go now

The Butterfly

ah, the sometime pain of being abandoned the sometime delight
         of singing
things that sometimes "oh oh," sometimes "aah aah," "ooh ooh"
the joy of frail things carrying the world on their shoulders
when the body of this joy flutters, tearing down boundaries,
the joyful shout issuing from the sometime pain of being
         abandoned, the sometime delight of singing the frailty
             of that shout
ah, the world shouldered by those sometime cries of aah aah
         oh oh ooh ooh
ah, the sometime feeling of haziness
hearts borne by weary bodies

Train Leaving

a train passes by and night flowers fall
night flowers fall, along with their traces
gone too alas is what I yearn for more than myself
but I stay and the train leaves
I remember your body inside mine
Ah, the things the body yearned for were already alike

YR

Na Hûidôk

(b. 1966)

Why I Write

There's a color that gets pinker and more lucid as time passes. It's the color of a glow in the sky. I saw it while zooming on the swing. I ardently desired to cross over to that world of color that summoned me, but my body on the swing always returned to the earth. The sky, without a glow, darkened again.

But there are moments when that glow seems to catch fire within me. When I think about poetry, when I write poetry, when I agonize over a poem to be written, one eye goes blind, another eye opens. I can't forsake poetry—probably because I wish to taste that agonizing rapture.

Burying their feet in the dirt, a monster called Chimera on their back,[1] bearing his weight pushing down, there are beings that jostle along somewhere. Baudelaire once confessed that instead of getting rid of that monster, he took on a heavier burden called "indifference." To me poetry comes into being when I, Chimera within me, yearn for another world, hanging onto the ropes of the swing. Oppressed by the weight of life and desire, the color of the sky as I look up is, to me, a poem.

---

1. Charles Baudelaire, "To Every Man his Chimera," in *Paris Spleen 1869*, translated by Louise Varese (New York: New Directions, 1970).

For Five Minutes

It seems my life will be spent
beneath this flower's shade,
waiting, pacing back and forth,
no, it may have already been spent—
five minutes waiting for a child
in the shade
of acacia flowers blowing white,
I've become an old woman.
When the bus turns the corner and stops in front of me,
it's not the six-year-old who hops down and hugs me
but a strapping youth who strides toward me—
as I grow older, he'll become an adult,
looking at me as if we've exchanged lives—
waiting, life passes in a flash—
I used to wait for him here, but
he won't be back for a long time.
Petals fall toward
the low tide of he who ebbed so far,
and I mumble to the passing bus and continue to wait.
While I mumble, a heap of petals falls again.
Look, here comes the bus!
I jump on it and out of the flowers' shade.

That Place Isn't Far

People who live outside of people
when they give up their breath
return for the first time inside people.

When a bird dies,
they lay their heads inside the bird.

Following the chirpings of their kin,
they stretch out their hearts,
but they can't fold their last wings.

One winter morning,
a fallen bird, without a wound,
on a forest path;

With the broad leaf of a silver magnolia
I cover that little sacred ground.

Dirty Nylons

The brown mare that ran until fatigued
is lying here
as if her weariness won't flow away.

Life is like a fine mesh stocking,
but even an awn's strands loosen—
knees and buttocks already sag.
Husk of desire removed,
my body, sagging all over,
still recalls its curves,
like a *p'ansori* singer's empty dress.
How strange my bare feet look!
I pick them up and plop them in water;
a long busy day is developing.

The mare drank some water
and rose; its browness, deepened,
became another coat.

Like a dragonfly's wings beating all night long,
it won't take long to dry.

Women Within Me

Within me a half-veined magnolia,
a sharp-needled white pine tree,
several peonies with curled leaves,
early-blossoming lilacs
now fated to be thick with leaves.

Women like these live within me.
Settling on a patch of soil,
putting down roots,
I hoped they'd grab my soul's ankle
and be unable to leave,
pretending not to listen to wind,
whose pitch was too high or too low.
Some days, I took pruning shears
and randomly trimmed the thick branches,
pricking my hand with a leaf's tip.
On such nights
the roots inside me, those women, suffered fatigue.

When on a spring day in other gardens
dozens of blossoms open like fireworks,
a single magnolia in my garden barely comes into bloom,
a few raindrops gathered in the peony's closed leaves sowly dry,
and the scattered fragrance of lilacs has not returned,
wind passing my garden pretends not to notice.

Like the Vineyard

I'd live like that low vineyard
bending my body below the ridge,
lying low, low,
as if hidden, but not wholly.
I've something to ripen in the outside world,
a single word left inside my mouth;
I hold it like a grape seed,
I don't want to disclose,
a dream to wrap around this body and bury myself in—
a dream I had behind a bouquet of leaves

I may be a grape thrown into the world's wine barrel,
and crushed, unripe, into juice to become a mouthful of words—
I may no longer be round,
and be splashing as something other than a grape,
or as a fragrance, be another spreading rumor,
that's moistening the world—

The peace of the low-lying vineyard.
As if I were still hanging on the vine,
I trace my lost body with a lost hand,
as if I knew how to make it ripen secretly!

Song of Grass

Until your source dries up,
give me a hard cascade, oh waterfall!
I'd like to be beaten by your whip,
with no time to rise again,
no chance to complain of my pain,
beat down.
I'll answer only with my cries,
striking roots between these rocks.
I see you, but if you blind my eyes,
I won't mind becoming a blue bruise. . . .

How sore, too, your body must be!

A Cold Rain Comes

—Letter I

The glowing blossoms we tended together
say they have pain pain pain
from last night's cold rain.
But I can't be sick,
or you'll get hurt.
Raindrops that flow down the eaves
all night long are like that;
the last drop can't bear to fall
and remains suspended in air.
To fall, to wither,
those that are suspended,
are they dazzling
because of their sorrow's weight?
This foreboding of an awful illness,
is it something like the fragrance
of flowers just before they fall?
I can't be fragrant fervently
or you'll get hurt.

Sleeping on the Nail

Small swallow's nest under the eaves
filled with fledglings—
mother bird covers the nest with her wings
and barely falls asleep.
Just there someone drove a nail.
Were it not for this nail,
where would father bird spend the night?
I gaze intently at the bird settled on the nail.
He nods all through the night.
A bus stop at Chongam Street
where a dusty wind blows;
a man with three children are there to meet someone.
After many buses,
a work-worn woman gets off,
her wan face making the half-moon more pale.
The children dash to their mother, clinging to her skirt,
the man remains standing, looking at the moon—
I seem able to read his mind tonight.
The jobless man fumbles with dirty walnuts
in his pockets that won't easily crack—
instead of building a so-called house,
father bird managed to live on the nail!
A dusty wind still drives down the street.
On their way home, dim moonlight made
shadows of the family clasping each other's hands
in a lane too narrow for them to walk abreast.
The shadow of the father walks a step behind,
making me recall the single nail,
the nodding bird, sleeping on the nail.

There's Such an Evening

Toward dusk
a stream's ripples glimmer without reflecting
the last confusion of dayflies tangled
in the sky's corner—
on certain days I dare look at such things.

The sound of hot earth cooling its body,
the sound of blue winds passing by,
the sound of flowers on the bank closing their mouths—
on certain days I dare listen to such things.

While darkness comes, effacing light,
I try to stand there quietly
putting a ring around my body
until a darkness that can't escape
embeds itself like a node.

The road of long ago is broken,
and there's such an evening when
I want to stand before a thick grove.

Five A.M.

The one who comes with a broom,
what does he sweep away at dawn?
The sound of sweeping inside my brain,
the sound of my heart being cut out.
Every dawn he cried by my pillow,
but I never heard him.
Though stars in the sky still glistened,
the sweeping sounds should have awakened me,
but as though the alarm had not been set—I slept!

PL

BIOGRAPHICAL NOTES

Yi Hyangji

Born on 16 December 1942 in Ch'ungmu, South Kyôngsang, Yi Hyangji graduated from Pusan University in 1967 and made her literary debut in 1989. The author of two volumes of poetry (1992, 1995), she is married and has one son and one daughter.

Poetry

Kwarho soge kwittûrami (A cricket inside a parenthesis). Hyôndae segyesa, 1992.
Kujôlli param sori (Sounds of winds at Kujôlli). Segyesa, 1995.
Muri kanûn kilgwa parami kanûn kil (The path where water passes and the path where wind passes). Nanam, 2001.

No Hyangnim

Born on 2 April 1942 in Haenam, South Chôlla, No Hyangnim graduated from Chungang University in English Literature. She made her debut in 1970. She is married with one son and is a full-time homemaker. In 1987 she received the literature prize from the Republic of Korea.

Poetry

K ûp kihaeng (A trip to K village). Hyôndae munhaksa, 1977.
Yônsûpki rûl ttiugo (After flying a trainer). Yônhûi ch'ulp'ansa, 1980.
Nuni oji annûn nara (A country where no snow falls). Munhak sasangsa, 1987.
Kûrium i ômnûn saramûn Ap'aedo rûl poji mothanda (One without longing cannot see Ap'ae Island). Munhak sasangsa, 1992.
Hut'ut'i ka ojiannûn sôm (Island wrens never visit). Ch'angjak kwa pip'yôngsa, 1998.

Essays

Ap'ûm kkaji saranghalsu innûn sarang i arûmdapsûmnida (Love that can love pain is beautiful). Hangyôrae, 1992.

Ch'ôn Yanghûi

Born on 21 January 1942 in Pusan, Ch'ôn graduated from Ehwa Woman's University in Korean literature (1966). She made her debut in 1965 and won the 10th Sowôl Poetry Prize (1995). She was divorced in 1973 and has one son.

Poetry

Sin i uir ege munnûn tamyôn (If god asks us). P'yôngminsa, 1983.
Saram kûriun tosi (A city that longs for people). Nanam, 1988.
Haruch'i ûi hûimang (Hope of one day's portion). Ch'ôngha, 1992.
Maûm ûi susubat (A millet field in my mind). Ch'angjak kwa pip'yôngsa, 1994.
Toksinnyô ege (To the single woman). Munhak sasang, 1997.
Oraedoen kolmok (An old alley). Ch'angjak kwa pip'yôngsa, 1998.
Kûrium ûn toragal chariga ôpta: siro ssûn yônghon ûi chasôjôn (Longing has no place to return: A soul's poetic autobiography). Chakka chôngsin, 1998.

Essays

Muso ûi ppul ch'ôrôm hollo kara (Go alone like a rhinoceros' horn). Tungji, 1989.

Sarang poda sojunghan haengbok ûn ôpta (No happiness is more precious than love). T'obang, 1990.

Sarami toeôyaji mwôga p'iryohae (You should become a human being—what else do you need?). Uri munhaksa,1998.

Hayan tarûi yôsin (The white moon goddess). Hanûl yônmot, 1999.

KANG ÛNGYO

Born on 13 December 1945 in Hongwôn, South Hamgyông, Kang Ûngyo grew up in Seoul. She graduated from Yonsei University in English literature (1968) and continued her study in the graduate school. She made her debut in 1968 with a prize from the journal *Sasanggye*. The author of twelve volumes of poetry or selected poems, thirteen volumes of prose, and three translations, currently she is professor of Korean literature at Tonga University in Pusan. Divorced, she has one daughter.

Poetry

Hômu chip (Anthology of nothingness). Ch'ilsimnyôndae tonginhoe, 1971.

P'ullip (Leaves of grass). Minûmsa, 1974.

Pinja ilgi (A pauper's diary). Minûmsa, 1977.

Sori chip (Collection of sounds). Ch'angjak kwa pip' yôngsa, 1982.

Pulgûn kang (Red river). P'ulpit, 1984.

Uri ga muri toeyô (We become water). Munhak sasangsa, 1986.

Param norae (Songs of winds). Munhak sasangsa, 1987.

Ônû miryu namu ûi saebyôk norae (Dawn song of a miryu tree). Tongmunsôn, 1988.

Onûl to nôrûl kidarinda (Waiting for you again today). Silch'ôn munhaksa, 1989.

Pyôk sogûi p'yônji (Letters inside the wall). Ch'angjak kwa pip'yôngsa, 1992.

Ônû pyôl esoûi haru (A day in a star). Ch'angjak kwa pip'yôngsa, 1996.

Sarang pinûl (Scales of love). Chohûn nal, 1998.

Tûngppul hanaga kôrô onae (A lamp is walking towad me). Munhak tongnae, 1999.

Kajang k'ûn hanûrûn ônjena kûdae tûng twie itta (The biggest sky is always over your shoulder). Ch'ajûlmo, 1999.

Essays

Ch'uôk che (Feast of memory). Minûmsa, 1975.

Kûmul sairo (Caught in the net). Chisik sanôpsa, 1975.

Tosi ûi aidûl (Children of the city). Chinmun ch'ulp'ansa, 1977.

Siin such'ôp (Poet's notebook). Munye ch'ulp'ansa, 1977.

Uri ka muri toeyô mannan tamyôn (If we become water and meet). Saebyôk ch'ulp'ansa, 1979.

Sarang ûi purûl nohûrira (I'll set love on fire). Saebyôk ch'ulp'ansa, 1980.

Nuga p'urip ûro tasi nûn ttûrya (Who will spring up again like the grass?). Munhak segye sa, 1984.

Ôduuni pyôl ttûnûn hanûl i inne (There is a sky where stars rise when darkness falls). Yôngôn munhwasa, 1985.

Sullyeja ûi kkum (A pilgrim's dream). Nanam ch'ulp'ansa, 1988.

Hana ûi ôlgul ûl wihayo (For the sake of one face). Tongmunsôn, 1988.

Chamdûlmyônsô ch'amûro chamdûlchi mothamyônsô (Falling asleep, truly unable to fall asleep). Hanyang ch'ulp'ansa, 1993.

Hômu such'ôp (Notebook of emptiness). Yejônsa, 1996.

Talp'aengi ka tallilttae: ttarege chunûn p'yônji (When the snail runs: Letters to my daughter). Saemt'ô, 1998.

Chôlmûn siin ege ponaenûn p'yônji (Letters to a young poet). Munhak tongnae, 2000.

Translations

Nikos Kazantazakis, The Saviors of God: Spiritual Exercises (1927; tr. 1960). Wôrinjae, 1981.

Henry David Thoreau. Irae, 1999.

Mun Chônghui

Born on 25 May 1947 in Posông, South Chôlla, Mun graduated from Tongguk University in 1970 and received her doctorate, with a dissertation on the poetry of Sô Chôngju, from Seoul Women's University (1992). In 1995 she took part in the International Writing Program at the University of Iowa. Making her debut in 1969, Mun is the author of fifteen volumes of poetry or selected poems and four volumes of essays. She is a recipient of the prize from the journal *Hyôndae munhak* (1976) and the Sowôl Poetry Prize (1996). Married in 1969, she has one son and one daughter. Currently she is teaching poetry writing at Tongguk University.

Poetry

Kkotsum (Breath of flowers). Hanguk chongp'ansa, 1963.

Mun Chônghûi sijip (Collection of Mun Chônghûi's poems). Wôlgan munhaksa, 1973.

Saettae (Flock of birds). Munhaksa, 1975.

Honja munôjinûn chongsori (Crumbling sound of a bell). Munhak yesulsa, 1984.

Tchille (Wild Rose). Chônyewôn, 1985.

Aunaeûi sae (Bird in my younger sister's home). Irwôl sôgak, 1986.

Kûriun naûi sôm (An island I long for). Yejônsa, 1987.

Hanûl poda môngose maein kûnae (Swing at a place further away than sky). Nanam, 1988.

Kkumkkunûn nunssôp (Dreaming eyelids). Sinwôn munhwasa, 1989.

Che momsoge salgo innûn saerûl kkônaejuseyo (Please remove the bird nesting inside my body). Tulkkôt sesang, 1990.

Pyôri ttûmyôn sûlp'um to hyanggiropta (Sorrow too is fragrant when stars are out). Mihaksa, 1993.

Namja rûl wihayô (For the man). Minûmsa, 1996.

Sap'o ûi ch'ôtsarang (First love of Sappho). Segyesa, 1998.

I sesang modûn sarangûn mujoe ida (All the world's love is guilt-free). Ûlp'aso, 1999.

Essays

Chôlmun konoe wa sarang (Young love and anguish). Kwandong ch'ulp'ansa, 1976.

Ch'ôngch'un ûi mihak (Aesthetic of youth). Kwandong ch'ulp'ansa, 1980.

Uri yônghon ûi amhomun hana (A cryptogram of our soul). Munhak sasangsa, 1987.

Tangdanghan yôja (Magnificent woman). Tungji, 1992.

Nunmul (Tears). Chiphyônjôn, 1997.

Paraponûn kônmanûrodo nan haengbok hada (I'm happy watching). Munhak p'unggyông, 1999.

Miwan ûi kido (Unfinished prayer). Saemi, 2000.

YI KYÔNGNIM

Born on 30 July 1947 in Mungyông, North Kyôngsang, Yi made her debut in 1989. The author of three volumes of poetry, she is married in 1969 with one son and two daughters. Since 1992, she has been a lecturer at a private educational institution.

Poetry

T'ossi ch'akki (Searching for particles). Paeksong, 1992.

Kûgosedo sagôri nûn itta (A crossroads even there). Segyesa, 1995.

Sijôl hana onda, chabamôkcha (A season is coming, let's devour it). Ch'angjak kwa pip'yôngsa, 1997.

KO CHÔNGHÛI

Poetry

Nuga hollo sult'ûrûl palko innûnga (Who's squeezing the wine press alone?). P'yôngminsa, 1985.

Sillagwôn kihaeng (A trip to paradise lost). Inmundang, 1981.

Ch'ohonje (Ritual to call back the soul). Ch'angjak kwa pip'yôngsa, 1983.

Isidae ûi abel (Abel of this age). Munhak kwa chisôngsa, 1983.

Nunmul kkot (Flowers of tears). Silch'ôn munhaksa, 1986.

Chirisan ûi pom (Spring on Mount Chiri). Munhak kwa chisôngsa, 1987.

Chô mudômwi ûi p'urûn chandi (Green grass on that grave). Ch'angjak kwa pip'yôngsa, 1989.

Kwangju ûi nunmulbi (Tears falling on Kwangju).

Yôsông haebang ch'ulsap'yo (Declaration for the campaign for women's liberation). Tonggwang ch'ulp'ansa, 1990.

Arûmdaun saram hana (A beautiful person). Tûlkkot sesang, 1991.

Posthumous work

Modu sarajinun kôttûrûn twie yôbaegûl namginda (All that vanishes leaves a blank). Ch'angjak kwa pip'yôngsa, 1992.

CH'OE SÛNGJA

Born on 25 May 1952 Ch'oe studied German literature at Korea University (1971-75). She published four volumes of poetry and a volume of selected poems. In 1994, she took part in the International Writing Program at the University of Iowa. In 1995, her poems were published in Peru, where she read them, and also in Chile. She is the translator of some thirty volumes of English and American authors.

Poetry

I sidae ûi sarang (Love of this age). Munhak kwa chisôngsa, 1981.

Chûlgôun ilgi (Pleasant diary). Munhak kwa chisôngsa, 1984.
Kiôk ûi chip (House of memory). Munhak kwa chisôngsa, 1989.
Nae mudom p'urugo (My grave is green). Munhak kwa chisôngsa, 1993.
Yônindûl (Lovers). Munhak tongne, 1998.

Essays

Han keûrûn siin ui iyagi (Story of a lazy poet). Ch'aeksesang, 1990.
Ôttôn namudûrûn (Some trees). Segye, 1995.

Translations

Alan Paton. *Cry, the Beloved Country* (New York: C. Scribner's Sons, 1948).
  Hongsông, 1979.
Irving Stone. *Lust for Life: The Story of Vincent van Gogh* (New York: The Modern Library,
  1934). Ch'ôngha, 1980.
Alfred Alvarez. *The Savage God: A Study of Suicide* (London: Weidenfeld and Nicolson,
  1971). Ch'ôngha, 1981.
Friedrich Nietzsche. *Thus Spoke Zarathustra; A Book for All and None* (London: Penguin
  Books, 1978). Ch'ôngha, 1983.
Max Picard. *The World of Silence* (Chicago: H. Regnery, 1952). Kkach'i, 1985.
Edna St. Vincent Millay. *Collected Poems* (New York: Harper, 1956). Ch'ôngha, 1988.
Isabel Allende. *The House of the Spirits* (New York: A. A. Knopf, 1985). Tungji, 1990.
Richard Brautigan. *In Watermelon Sugar* (San Francisco: Four Seasons Foundation, 1968).
  Min, 1995.
Bharati Mukherjee. *Jasmine* (New York: Grove Weidenfeld, 1989). Munhak tongne,
  1996.
May Sarton. *Journal of a Solitude* (New York: Norton, 1973). Kkach'i, 1998.
Paul Auster. *The Art of Hunger: Essays, Prefaces, Interviews* (London: Menard Press, 1982).
  Munhak tongne, 1998.
David Fontana. *The Secret Language of Symbols; a Visual Key to Symbols and Their Meanings* (San
  Francisco: Chronicle Books, 1994). Munhak tongne, 1998.
Ted Hughes. *Birthday Letters* (London: Faber & Faber, 1998). Haenaem, 1999.
Gerald G. Jampolsky, *Out of Darkness into Light: A Journey of Inner Healing* (New York:
  Bantam Books, 1989). Ch'unhae taehak ch'ulp'anbu, 2000.

KIM SÛNGHÛI

Born on 1 March 1952, Kim received her B.A. (1974), M.A. (1981), and Ph.D. (1992), with a dissertation on the poetry of Yi Sang from Sôgang University. She was an instructor of Korean literature at her alma mater from 1982 to 1995, a visiting professor at the University of California, Berkeley (1996-97), and lecturer at the University of California, Irvine (1998-99). Currently she is professor of Korean literature at Sogang University.

Recipient of the Sowôl Poetry Prize in 1991, Kim has published seven volumes of poetry, five volumes of essays, and a novel. She is married and has one son and one daughter.

Poetry

T'aeyang misa (Sun worship). Koryôwôn, 1979.

Oenson ûl wihan hyôpchugok (Concerto for the left hand). Munhak sasangsa, 1983.

Miwansông ûl wihan yônga (Love song for the unfinished). Nanam, 1987.

Talgyal soge saeng (Life within an egg). Munhak sasangsa, 1989.

Ttôdonûn hwanyu (Floating metonymies). Munhak sasangsa, 1989.

Ôttôk'e pakkûro nagalkka (How to get out of this world?). Segyesa, 1992.

Nuga naûi sûlp'um ûl norajurya (Who will play my sorrow?). Miraesa, 1992.

Sesang esô kajang mugôun ssaum (The hardest battle in the world). Segyesa, 1995.

Pitcharu rûl t'ago tallinûn usûm (Laughing while riding a broom). Minûmsa, 2000.

Essays

Kodok ûl karik'inûn sigye panûl (A clock that teaches solitude). Kôryôwôn, 1980.

Pyôrang ûi norae (Songs of the cliff). Tongmunsôn, 1984.

Nôngma ro mandûn p'urûn kkot (Blue flower made from rags). Segyesa, 1990.

Sarang iranûn irûmûi susôngong (A repairman named love). Hanyang ch'ulp'ansa, 1995.

Nôrûl mannago sipta (I'd like to meet you). Ûngjin tak'ôm, 2000.

Fiction

Santap'e ro kanûn saram (One who goes to Santa Fe). Ch'angjak kwa pip'yôngsa, 1997.

Monographs

Yi Sang (Anthology of Yi Sang with biography). Munhak segyesa, 1993.

Yi Sang si yôngu (Studies in Yi Sang's poetry: semiotic approaches). Pogosa, 1998.

Kim Suyông tasi ilkki (Re-reading Kim Suyông). P'ûresû 21, 2000.

KIM CHÔNGNAN

Born in Seoul on 6 January 1953, Kim was graduated from Korean Foreign Language University in French, and in 1987 she received her doctorate from the University of Grenoble with a dissertation, "Le Pas de l'au-dela: La Quête initiatique chez Yves Bonnefoy." Since 1989, she has been professor of French at Sangji University in Wônju. She is the author of five volumes of poetry, two volumes of criticism, and translator of some ten volumes of French works. Married in December 1975, she has two sons.

Poetry

Tasi sijakhanûn nabi (A butterfly that flies again). Munhak kwa chisôngsa, 1989.

Maehok, hogûn kyôpch'im (Fascination, or folds). Segyesa, 1992.

Kû yôja, ipku esô kamanhi twidorabone (That woman looks back at the entrance). Segyesa, 1997.

Sût'ak'at'o nae yônghon (My staccato soul). Munye chungang, 1999.

Nanûn chigûm sarang ûl malhago itta (Now I speak of love). Yangp'iji, 1999.

Criticism

Piô innûn chungsim-miwan ûi sihak (Empty center—poetics of the unfinished). Ôno ûi segye, 1993.

Kôp'ûm araero kip'i (Deep under the foam). Saenggak ûi namu, 1998.

Translations

Nataf Georges. *Symboles, signes, et marques* (Paris: Berg, 1973). Yôrhwadang, 1987.

Jean Grenier. *Sur la mort d'un chien* (Paris: Gallimard, 1957). Ch'ôngha, 1987.

Jean Grenier. *Les grèves* (Paris: Gallimard, 1957). Ch'ôngha, 1991.

Jean-Yves Tadié. *La critique littéraire au Xe siècle* (P. Belfond: 1987). Munye ch'ulp'ansa, 1995.

Marcel Schneider. *Schubert* (Bourges: Editions du Seuil, 1957). Chungang ilbosa, 1995.

E. Harding. *Les mystières de la femme* (Paris: Payot 1953). Maunhak tongne, 1996.

Charles Jacques. *Ramses*, 5 volumes (Paris: Robert Lafont, 1996). Munhak tongne, 1997.

Christophe Bataille. *Le maître des heures* (Paris: Grasset et Fasquelle, 1997). Munhak tongne, 1997.

Ph. Delerme. *La première gorgée de la bière et autres plaisirs minuscules* (Paris: L'Arpenteur, 1997). Changnak, 1998.

J.P. Davidt. *Le petit prince retrouvé* (Montreal: Les Intouchables, 1997). Ire, 1998.

Michel Tournier. *Le miroir des idées* (Paris: Mercure de France, 1994). Hanttût, 1998.

Christian Bobin and Didier Cros, *Qelques jours avec elles* (Cognac: Le temp qu'il fait, 1994). Segyesa, 1998.

Yi Chinmyông

Born on 2 August 1955, Yi made her debut in 1990 and published two volumes of poetry (1992, 1994). Married in 1993, she has one daughter and is a full-time home-maker.

Poetry

Pame yongsô ranûn mal ûl tûrôtta (I heard the word "forgive" at night). Minûmsa, 1992.

Chibe toragal naltcharûl seôboda (Counting the days to go home). Manhak kwa chisôngsa, 1994.

Kim Hyesun

Born on 26 October 1955, she graduated from Kônguk University in Korean litera-ture and received a doctorate from the same university, with a dissertation on the poetry of Kim Suyông, in 1993. Currently she is a professor of Seoul Arts College. In addi-tion to five volumes of poetry, she is the author of two volumes of essays (1995, 1996) and a collection of fables (1990). Kim is married (1980) and has one daughter (b. 1982).

Kim is a recipient of the 1997 Kim Suyông Award, the 2000 Sowôl Poetry Prize, and contemporary poetry award (2000).

Poetry

Tto tarûn pyôl esô (From another star). Munhak kwa chisôngsa, 1981.

Abôji ka seun hôsuabi (Scarecrow my father built). Muhak kwa chisôngsa, 1984.

Ônû pyôl ûi chiok (Hell of a star). Ch'ôngha ch'ulp'ansa, 1987; reprint, Munhak tongue, 1997.

Uridûre ûmhwa (Our negative picture). Munhak kwa chisôngsa, 1991.

Naûi up'anisyadû Sôul (My Upanishad, Seoul). Munhak kwa chisôngsa, 1994.

Pulssanghan sarang kigye (A sad love machine). Munhak kwa chisôngsa, 1997.

Tallyôk kongjang kongjang changnim poseyo (To the calendar factory manager). Munhak kwa
   chisôngsa, 2000.
Prose
Tûlkkûllûn sarang (Swarming love: A trip to Spain). Hakkojae, 1996.
Kim Suyông: Segye ûi kaejin kwa chayu ûi ihaeng (Kim Suyông: progression of the world and
   shifting to freedom). Kônguk taehakkyo ch'ulp'anbu, 1995.

No Hyegyông
Born on 9 September 1958 in Pusan, currently she is completing her Ph.D. program
in Korean literature at Pusan University. She is married and has one daughter.
Poetry
Saeyôttôn kôsûl kiôk hanûn sae (A bird that remembers being a bird). Koryôwôn, 1995.
Ttûdômôkki chohûn ppang (Bread easy to eat). Segyesa, 1999.

Hwang Insuk
Born in Seoul on 21 December 1958, she graduated from Seoul Arts College in 1984.
Since her debut in 1984, she has published four volumes of poetry.
Poetry
Saenûn hanûrûl chayuropke p'urô nok'o (Birds freely loosen the sky). Munhak kwa chisôngsa,
   1988.
Sûlp'um i narûl kkaeunda (Sorrow wakes me). Munhak kwa chisôngsa, 1990.
Uri nûn ch'ôlsae ch'ôrôm mannatta (We met like seasonal birds). Munhak kwa chisôngsa,
   1994.
Naûi ch'imurhan sojunghan iyô (My gloomy valuable you). Munhak kwa chisôngsa, 1998.
Essays
Tchalpûn sarange kin pyônmyông (Long defense for brief love). Minûmsa, 1990.
Nanûn kodok hada (I'm lonely). Munhak tongne, 1997.

Chông Hwajin
Born on 10 November 1959 in Sangju, North Kyôngsang, she graduated from Korean
National Open University in French literature. She made her debut in 1986 and has
published two volumes of poetry. Married in 1990, she has two daughters and one son
and is a full-time homemaker.
Poetry
Changma nûn aidûrûl nun ttûge hago (Monsoon season opens children's eyes). Minûmsa,
1990.
Koyohan tongbaek ûl p'umûn padaga itta (There is a sea that embraces a quiet camellia).
   Minûmsa, 1994.

Yi Yônju
Poetry
Maeûmnyô ka innûn pame sijang (Night market with prostitutes). Segyesa, 1991.
Sokchoeyang yuda (Atoning sheep, Judas). Segyesa, 1993.

Yi Sanghûi

Born on 6 May 1960 in Pusan, she graduated from Pusan Women's University after majoring in Korean language (1982). She made her debut in 1987. Yi married in 1989 and has a daughter.

Poetry

Chal kara nae ch'ôngch'un (Farewell, my youth). Minûmsa, 1990.
Pyôrak munûi (Patterns of lightning). Minûmsa, 1998.

Fiction

Kkangt'ong (Empty can). Munhak tongnae, 2000.
Ch'uôk yôhaeng (Memory's journey). Tain midiô, 2000.

Pak Sôwôn

Born on 28 October 1960 in Seoul, Pak left Chônghwa Women's Commercial High School without graduating. She made her debut in 1989 and is the author of three volumes of poetry.

Poetry

Amudo ôpsoyô (There is no one). Yôrumsa, 1990.
Nangan wiûi koyangi (A cat on the rail). Segyesa, 1995.
I wanbyôkhan segye (This perfect world). Segyesa, 1997.

Prose

Ch'ônnyôn ûi kyôurûl kônnôon yôja (A woman who traversed a thousand years of winter). Tonga ilbosa, 1998.
Nae kiôk soge pin maûmûro saranghan tangsin (One I loved in my memory's emptiness). Segyesa, 1998.
Paengnyôn ûi sigan soge kach'in yôja (Woman imprisoned in a century). Chungang M&B, 2001.

Hô Sugyông

Born on 9 June 1964 in Chinju, South Kyôngsang, Hô graduated from Kyôngsang University in Korean literature (1986). She made her debut in 1987 and has published three volumes of poetry and a novel. Currently she is a graduate student of Near Eastern archaeology at the University of Münster, Germany.

Poetry

Sûlp'ûm manhan kôrûmi ôdi issûrya (Is there walking worthy of sorrow?). Silch'ôn munhak, 1988.
Honja kanûn mônjip (Going alone to a distant home). Munhak kwa chisôngsa, 1992.
Nae yônghonûn orae toessûna (My soul is aged, but). Ch'angjak kwa pip'yôngsa, 2001.

Fiction

Morae tosi (City of sand). Munhak tongne, 1996.

Na Hûidôk

Born on 8 February 1966 in Nonsan, South Ch'ungch'ông, she made her debut in 1989 and has published four volumes of poetry. After teaching the Korean language for seven years at a high school. Na is currently a doctoral candidate in modern Korean poetry at Yonsei University. She married in September 1989 and has a son and a daughter.

Poetry

Ppuri ege (To the root). Ch'angjak kwa pip'yôngsa, 1991

Kû mari ip'ûl multûryôtta (That word colored the leaves). Ch'angjak kwa pip'yôngsa, 1994.

Kûkosi môlji ant'a (That place is not far off). Minûmsa, 1997.

Ôduwôjindanûn kot (Getting dark). Ch'angjak kwa pip'yôngsa, 2001.

Prose

Pant'ong ûi mul (A half bucket of water). Ch'angjak kwa pip'yôngsa, 1999.